THE CRITICAL PATH

*An Essay on the Social Context
of Literary Criticism*

Northrop Frye

The Critical Path

*An Essay on the Social Context
of Literary Criticism*

INDIANA UNIVERSITY PRESS

Bloomington and London

FIRST MIDLAND BOOK EDITION 1973
Copyright © 1971 by Indiana University Press

Published in Canada by Fitzhenry & Whiteside Limited,
Don Mills, Ontario
Library of Congress catalog card number: 70-143246

253-31568-9 CL   253-20158-6 PA
Manufactured in the United States of America

Contents

Preface

This book is a farce, in the etymological sense: a fifty-minute lecture stuffed with its own implications until it swelled into the present monograph. In the spring of 1968, while visiting the Society for the Humanities at Cornell University, I gave a public lecture, which in turn engendered another lecture, "Mythos and Logos," given at the School of Letters in Indiana University that summer. These lectures form the basis of the present third and fourth sections, on the defence of poetry in Sidney and in Shelley. In the spring of 1969 I was visiting professor at Berkeley, on the Mrs. William Beckman foundation, and gave there two lectures which outlined the concern-and-freedom thesis. Meanwhile "student unrest" had been growing, and I was required to make several statements about it, of which the most relevant, to use *that* word, were addresses at Queen's University and at a conference at Quail Roost, Duke University, in the fall of 1968. These were published by, respectively, the Canadian Broadcasting Corporation and Tavistock Press, in books entitled *The Ethics of Change* and *Higher Education: Demand and Response* (both 1969), and parts of their arguments reappear here.

At that stage a long essay took shape, under its present title, which was contributed to a conference on the role of theory in humanistic studies held at Bellagio, Italy, in September, 1969, and published in the spring issue of *Daedalus* in 1970. During

7

this period I had been made an advisory member of the Canadian Radio and Television Commission, which had compelled me to think a certain amount about the relation of literary criticism to communication theory—somewhat unwillingly, as I had assumed that my colleague Professor Marshall McLuhan was taking care of that subject. Consistently with the main theme of this essay, the references to McLuhan in it are less about him than about the social stereotypes of McLuhanism. After the essay had appeared in *Daedalus,* and after I had given a number of lectures in places as far apart as Southern California and Pakistan, I revised and expanded it to about twice its size, adopting, after some inner resistance, a more historical method of exposition, of a type I often find facile, but which seemed to be right for this argument. I then began what I assumed would be a brief and perfunctory revision, and found myself completely rewriting the book again. This last operation took place at Oxford, and I am deeply grateful to the Association of Commonwealth Universities, and to the Warden and Fellows of Merton College, for conspiring to provide me with such pleasant conditions of work. During this time I chopped out part of the sixth section for a BBC talk on communications, reprinted in *The Listener.*

I also owe much more than I can express here to a great number of other people. I think first of the hosts at my various lectures, whose encouragement and hospitality meant so much; then of a good many members of the FILLM conference in Pakistan and of practically everybody at the Bellagio conference; then of many students and staff who attended my lectures and asked questions and made objections. They have been responsible for a few additions, and for many deletions and modifications. It is only because of such friendly interest, often coming from people whose names I did not get, that the list of "Faults Escaped," if long, is perhaps not interminable.

In a sense most of the main points in this book have been expounded elsewhere in other connexions. I reflect however that a writer has increasingly less that is radically new to say unless he has previously been wrong. One of my less perceptive reviewers remarked recently that I seemed to be rewriting my central myth in every book I produced. I certainly do, and would never read or trust any writer who did not also do so. But one hopes for some growth in lucidity, or at least an increase of the presbyopia that normally comes in later life, as one proceeds.

N. F.

Massey College
Victoria College
University of Toronto
July, 1970.

Acknowledgments

Acknowledgment is made to *Daedalus* for permission to reprint, in much expanded form, an essay originally published in their pages. Acknowledgment is also made to the School of Letters of Indiana University for permission to reprint an earlier version of the same essay which appeared in their anniversary booklet. Some sentences in the sixth section, as noted, are reproduced in *Higher Education: Demand and Response* (1969), though the version here is generally the earlier one.

THE CRITICAL PATH

*An Essay on the Social Context
of Literary Criticism*

One

The phrase "The Critical Path" is, I understand, a term in business administration, and was one that I began hearing extensively used during the preparations for the Montreal Expo of 1967. It associated itself in my mind with the closing sentences of Kant's *Critique of Pure Reason*, where he says that dogmatism and skepticism have both had it as tenable philosophical positions, and that "the critical path is alone open." It also associated itself with a turning point in my own development. About twenty-five years ago, when still in middle life, I lost my way in the dark wood of Blake's prophecies, and looked around for some path that would get me out of there. There were many paths, some well trodden and equipped with signposts, but all pointing in what for me were the wrong directions. They directed me to the social conditions of Blake's time, to the history of the occult tradition, to psychological factors in Blake's mind, and other subjects quite valid in themselves. But my task was the specific one of trying to crack Blake's symbolic code, and I had a feeling that the way to that led directly through literature itself. The critical path I wanted was a theory of criticism which would, first, account for the major phenomena of literary experience, and, second, would lead to some view of the place of literature in civilization as a whole.

Following the bent that Blake had given me, I became particularly interested in two questions. One was: What is the total subject of study of which criticism forms part? I rejected the answer: "Criticism is a subdivision of literature," because it was such obvious nonsense. Criticism is the theory of literature, not a minor and non-essential element in its practice. This latter notion of it is not surprising in outsiders, or in poets, but how a critic himself can be so confused about his function as to take the same view I could not (and cannot yet) understand. Of course criticism has a peculiar disability in the number of people who have drifted into it without any vocation for it, and who may therefore have, however unconsciously, some interest in keeping it theoretically incoherent.

Literary criticism in its turn seemed to be a part of two larger but undeveloped subjects. One was the unified criticism of all the arts; the other was some area of verbal expression which had not yet been defined, and which in the present book is called mythology. The latter seemed more immediately promising: the former I felt was the ultimate destiny of the subject called aesthetics, in which (at least at that time) relatively few technically competent literary critics appeared to be much interested. I noticed also the strong centrifugal drift from criticism toward social, philosophical and religious interests, which had set in at least as early as Coleridge. Some of this seemed to me badly motivated. A critic devoting himself to literature, but without any sense of his distinctive function, is often tempted to feel that he can never be anything more than a second-class writer or thinker, because his work is derived from the work of what by his postulates are greater men. I felt, then, that a conception of criticism was needed which would set the critic's activity in its proper light, and that once we had that, a critic's other interests would represent a natural expansion of criticism rather than an escape from it.

The other question was: How do we arrive at poetic meaning? It is a generally accepted principle that meaning is derived from context. But there are two contexts for verbal meaning: the imaginative context of literature, and the context of ordinary intentional discourse. I felt that no critic had given his full attention to what seemed to me to be the first operation of criticism: trying to see what meaning could be discovered in works of literature from their context in literature. All meaning in literature seemed to be referred first of all to the context of intentional meaning, always a secondary and sometimes the wrong context. That is, the primary meaning of a literary work was assumed to be the kind of meaning that a prose paraphrase could represent. This primary meaning was called the "literal" meaning, a phrase with a luxuriant growth of semantic tangles around it which I have discussed elsewhere and return to more briefly here.

When I first began to write on critical theory, I was startled to realize how general was the agreement that criticism had no presuppositions of its own, but had to be "grounded" on some other subject. The disagreements were not over that, but over the question of what the proper subjects were that criticism ought to depend on. The older European philological basis, a very sound one, at least in the form in which it was expounded by August Boeckh and others in the nineteenth century, had largely disappeared in English-speaking countries. In some places, notably Oxford, where I studied in the thirties, it had declined into a much narrower conception of philology. This was partly because the shifting of the centre of literary study from the Classical to the modern languages had developed a prejudice, derived from one of the more bizarre perversions of the work ethic, that English literature at least was a merely entertaining subject, and should not be admitted to universities unless the main emphasis fell on something more beneficial to the moral fibre, like learning the classes of Old English strong verbs. In most North American universities the critical establishment rested on a mixture of history and philosophy, evidently on the assumption that every work of literature is what Sir Walter Raleigh said *Paradise Lost* was, a monument to dead ideas. I myself was soon identified as one of the critics who took their assumptions from anthropology and psychology, then still widely regarded as the wrong subjects. I have always insisted that criticism cannot take presuppositions from elsewhere, which always means wrenching them out of their real context, and must work out its own. But mental habits are hard to break, especially bad habits, and, because I found the term "archetype" an essential one, I am still often called a Jungian critic, and classified with Miss Maud Bodkin, whose book I have read with interest, but whom, on the evidence of that book, I resemble about as closely as I resemble the late Sarah Bernhardt.

The reason for this rather silly situation was obvious enough. As long as the meaning of a poem, let us say for short, is sought primarily within the context of intentional discourse, it becomes a document, to be related to some verbal area of study outside literature. Hence criticism, like Los Angeles, becomes an aggregate of suburbs, with no central area in literature itself. One of these suburbs is the biographical one, where the literary work is taken to be a document illustrating something in the writer's life. The most fashionable time for this approach was the nineteenth century, and its strongest proponent Carlyle, for whom great poetry could only be the personal rhetoric of a great man. The theory demands that Shakespeare, for instance, should be an obviously and over-whelmingly great man, which is why so much nineteenth-century critical energy was expended in trying to invent a sufficiently interesting biography for Shakespeare out of fancied allusions in the poetry. This misguided industry has now largely been restricted to the sonnets, where, as Mutt says in *Finnegans Wake,* "he who runes may rede it on all fours." Carlyle's essay on Shakespeare, in *Heroes and Hero-Worship,* comes as close to pure verbiage, to rhetoric without content, as prose sentences can in the nature of things get. Something seems to be wrong with the theory, at least in this form. One is better off with Goethe, but even there the sense of personal greatness may be connected less with the quality of the poetry than with the number of things Goethe had been able to do besides writing poetry.

I am not talking here about real biography, but about the assumption that the poet's life is the essential key to the deeper understanding of the poetry. It often happens that interesting literature is produced by an uninteresting man, in the sense of one who disappoints us if we are looking for some kind of culture-hero. In fact it happens so often that there is clearly no correlation between the ability to write poetry and any other ability, or, at least, it is clearly absurd to assume that every real poet must be a certain kind of person. Hence the formula "this poem is particularly notable for the way in which it throws light on," etc., soon ceases to carry much conviction for all but a selected group of poets. Something else, more deeply founded in a wider literary experience, is needed for critical understanding.

In these days, a biographical approach is likely to move from the manifest to the latent personal content of the poem, and from a biographical approach properly speaking to a psychological one. At the present time and place this means very largely a Freudian, or what I think of as a Luther-on-the-privy, approach. A considerable amount of determinism enters at this stage. All documentary conceptions of literature are allegorical conceptions of it, and this fact becomes even more obvious when poems are taken to be allegories of Freudian repressions, unresolved conflicts, or tensions between ego and id, or, for another school, of the Jungian process of individuation. But what is true of allegorical poetry is equally true of allegorical criticism: that allegory is a technique calling for tact. Tact is violated when the whiteness of Moby Dick is explained as a Lockian *tabula rasa,* or when Alice in Wonderland is discussed in terms of her hypothetical toilet training, or when Matthew Arnold's line in *Dover Beach,* "Where ignorant armies clash by night," is taken as a covert reference to the copulation of his parents. One is reminded of the exempla from natural history made by medieval preachers. According to Richard Rolle in the fourteenth century, the bee carries earth in its feet to ballast itself when it flies, and thereby reminds us of the Incarnation, when God took up an earthly form. The example is ingenious and entertaining, and only unsatisfying if one happens to be interested in bees.

If we tire of the shadow-play of explaining real poems by assumed mental states, we may be driven to realize that the ultimate source of a poem is not so much the individual poet as the social situation from which he springs, and of which he is the spokesman and the medium. This takes us into the area of historical criticism. Here again no one can or should deny the relevance of literature to history, but only rarely in historical criticism is there any real sense of the fact that literature is itself an active part of the historical process. Poets are assumed to have a sensitive litmus-paper response to social trends, hence literature as a whole is taken to be something that the historical process acts on, and we have still not escaped from a documentary and allegorical procedure.

Once more, some historical critics, like the biographical ones, will want to go from manifest to latent social content, from the historical context of the poem to its context in some unified overview of history. Here again determinism, the impulse to find the ultimate meaning of literature in something that is not literature, is unmistakable. At the time of which I am speaking, a generation ago, a conservative Catholic determinism was fashionable, strongly influenced by Eliot, which adopted Thomism, or at least made references to it, as the summit of Western cultural values, and looked down benignantly on everything that followed it as a kind of toboggan slide, rushing through nominalism, Protestantism, liberalism, subjective idealism, and so on to the solipsism in which the critic's non-Thomist contemporaries were assumed to be enclosed. Marxism is another enlarged historical perspective, widely adopted, and perhaps inherently the most serious one of them all. Literature is a part of a social process; hence that process as a whole forms the genuine context of literature. Theoretically, Marxism takes a social view of literature which is comprehensive enough to see it within this genuine context. In practice, however, Marxism operates as merely one more determinism, which avoids every aspect of literature except one allegorical interpretation of its content.

All these documentary and external approaches, even when correctly handled, are subject to at least three limitations which every experienced scholar has to reckon with. In the first place, they do not account for the literary form of what they are discussing. Identifying Edward King and documenting Milton's attitude to the Church of England will throw no light on *Lycidas* as a pastoral elegy with specific Classical and Italian lines of ancestry. Secondly, they do not account for the poetic and metaphorical language of the literary work, but assume its primary meaning to be a non-poetic meaning. Thirdly, they do not account for the fact that the genuine quality of a poet is often in a negative relation to the chosen context. To understand Blake's *Milton* and *Jerusalem* it is useful to know something of his quarrel with Hayley and his sedition trial. But one also needs to be aware of the vast disproportion between these minor events in a quiet life and their apocalyptic transformation in the poems. One should also know enough of criticism, as well as of Blake, not to ascribe the disproportion to paranoia on Blake's part. Similarly, a scholar may write a whole shelf of books about the life of Milton studied in connexion with the history of his time, and still fail to notice that Milton's greatness as a poet has a good deal to do with his profound and perverse misunderstanding of the history of his time.

By the time I begun writing criticism, the so-called "new criticism" had established itself as a technique of explication. This was a rhetorical form of criticism, and from the beginning rhetoric has meant two things: the figuration of language and the persuasive powers of an orator. New criticism dealt with rhetoric in the former sense, and established a counterweight to the biographical approach which treated poetry as a personal rhetoric. The great merit of explicatory criticism was that it accepted poetic language and form as the basis for poetic meaning. On the basis it built up a resistance to all "background" criticism that explained the literary in terms of the non-literary. At the same time, it deprived itself of the great strength of documentary criticism: the sense of context. It simply explicated one work after another, paying little attention to genre or to any larger structural principles connecting the different works explicated.

The limitations of this approach soon became obvious, and

most of the new critics sooner or later fell back on one of the established documentary contexts, generally the historical one, although they were regarded at first as anti-historical. One or two have even been Marxists, but in general the movement, at least in America, was anti-Marxist. Marxists had previously condemned the somewhat similar tendency in Russian criticism called "formalism," because they realized that if they began by conceding literary form as the basis for literary significance, the assumptions on which Marxist bureaucracies rationalized their censorship of the arts would be greatly weakened. They would logically have to end, in fact, in giving poets and novelists the same kind of freedom that they had reluctantly been compelled to grant to the physical scientists.

More recently, Marshall McLuhan has placed a formalist theory, expressed in the phrase "the medium is the message," within the context of a neo-Marxist determinism in which communication media play the same role that instruments of production do in more orthodox Marxism. Professor McLuhan drafted his new mosaic code under a strong influence from the conservative wing of the new critical movement, and many traces of an earlier Thomist determinism can be found in *The Gutenberg Galaxy*. An example is the curiously exaggerated distinction he draws between the manuscript culture of the Middle Ages and the book culture of the printed page that followed it.

It seemed to me obvious that, after accepting the poetic form of a poem as its primary basis of meaning, the next step was to look for its context within literature itself. And of course the most obvious literary context for a poem is the entire output of its author. Just as explication, by stressing the more objective aspect of rhetoric, had formed a corrective to the excesses of biographical criticism, so a study of a poet's whole work might form the basis of a kind of "psychological" criticism that would operate within literature, and so provide some balance for the kind that ends in the bosom of Freud. Poetry is, after all, a technique of communication: it engages the conscious part of the mind as well as the murkier areas, and what a poet succeeds in communicating to others is at least as important as what he fails to resolve for himself.

We soon become aware that every poet has his own distinctive structure of imagery, which usually emerges even in his earliest work, and which does not and cannot essentially change. This larger context of the poem within its author's entire "mental landscape" is assumed in all the best explication—Spitzer's, for example. I became aware of its importance myself, when working on Blake, as soon as I realized that Blake's special symbolic names and the like did form a genuine structure of poetic imagery and not, despite his use of the word, a "system" to which he was bound like an administrator to a computer. The structure of imagery, however, as I continued to study it, began to show an increasing number of similarities to the structures of other poets. Blake had always been regarded as a poet with a "private symbolism" locked up in his own mind, but this conception of him was so fantastically untrue that overcoming it carried me much further than merely correcting a mistaken notion of Blake.

I was led to three conclusions in particular. First, there is no private symbolism: the phrase makes no sense. There may be private allusions or associations that need footnotes, but they cannot form a poetic structure, even if the poet himself is a psychotic. The structure of the poem remains an effort at communication, however utterly it may fail to communicate. Second, as just said, every poet has his own structure of imagery, every detail of which has its analogue in that of all other poets. Third, when we follow out this pattern of analogous structures, we find that it leads, not to similarity, but to identity. Similarity implies uniformity and monotony, and any conclusion that all poets are much alike, in whatever respect, is too false to our literary experience to be tenable. It is identity that makes individuality possible: poems are made out of the *same* images, just as poems in English are all made out of the same language. This contrast of similarity and identity is one of the most difficult problems in critical theory, and we shall have to return to it several times in this book.

I was still not satisfied: I wanted a historical approach to literature, but an approach that would be or include a genuine history of literature, and not simply the assimilating of literature to some other kind of history. It was at this point that the immense importance of certain structural elements in the literary tradition, such as conventions, genres, and the recurring use of certain images or image-clusters, which I came to call archetypes, forced itself on me. T. S. Eliot had already spoken of tradition as a creative and informing power operating on the poet specifically as a craftsman, and not vaguely as a merely cultivated person. But neither he nor anyone else seemed to get to the point of identifying the factors of that tradition, of what it is that makes possible the creation of new works of literature out of earlier ones. The new critics had resisted the background approach to criticism, but they had not destroyed the oratorical conception of poetry as a personal rhetoric.

And yet convention, within literature, seemed to be a force even stronger than history. The difference between the conventions of medieval poets writing in the London of Richard II and those of Cavalier poets writing in the London of Charles II is far less than the difference in social conditions between the two ages. I began to suspect that a poet's relation to poetry was much more like a scholar's relation to his scholarship than was generally thought. Whatever one is producing, the psychological processes involved seem much the same. The scholar cannot be a scholar until he immerses himself in his subject, until he attaches his own thinking to the body of what is thought in his day about that subject. A scholar, *qua* scholar, cannot think for himself or think at random: he can only expand an organic body of thought, add something logically related to what he or someone else has already thought. But this is precisely the way that poets have always talked about their relation to poetry. From Homer onward, poets have continually insisted that they were simply places where something new in literature was able to take its own shape.

From here it is clear that one has to take a final step. Criticism must develop a sense of history within literature to complement the historical criticism that relates literature to its non-literary historical background. Similarly, it must develop its own form of historical overview, on the basis of what is inside literature rather than outside it. Instead of fitting literature into a prefabricated scheme of history, the critic should see literature as a coherent structure, historically conditioned but shaping its own history, responding to but not determined in its form by an external historical process. This total body of literature can be studied through its larger structural principles, which I have just described as conventions, genres and recurring image-groups or archetypes. These structural principles are largely ignored by most social critics. Their treatment of literature, in consequence, is usually superficial, a matter of picking things out of literary works that seem interesting for non-literary reasons.

When criticism develops a proper sense of the history of literature, the history beyond literature does not cease to exist or to be relevant to the critic. Similarly, seeing literature as a unity in itself does not withdraw it from a social context: on the contrary, it becomes far easier to see what its place in civilization is. Criticism will always have two aspects, one turned toward the structure of literature and one turned toward the other cultural phenomena that form the social environment of literature. Together, they balance each other: when one is worked on to the exclusion of the other, the critical perspective goes out of focus. If criticism is in proper balance, the tendency of critics to move from critical to larger social issues becomes more intelligible. Such a movement need not, and should not, be due to a dissatisfaction with the narrowness of criticism as a discipline, but should be simply the result of a sense of social context, a sense present in all critics from whom one is in the least likely to learn anything.

There was another difficulty with new criticism which was only a technical one, but still pointed to the necessity for a sense of context. Whenever we read anything there are two mental operations we perform, which succeed one another in time. First we follow the narrative movement in the act of reading, turning over the pages and pursuing the trail from top left to bottom right. Afterwards, we can look at the work as a simultaneous unity and study its structure. This latter act is the critical response properly speaking: the ordinary reader seldom needs to bother with it. The chief material of rhetorical analysis consists of a study of the poetic "texture," and such a study plunges one into a complicated labyrinth of ambiguities, multiple meanings, recurring images, and echoes of both sound and sense. A full explication of a long and complex work which was based on the reading process could well become much longer, and more difficult to read, than the work itself. Such linear explications have some advantages as a teaching technique, but for publishing purposes it is more practicable to start with the second stage. This involves attaching the rhetorical analysis to a deductive framework derived from a study of the structure, and the context of that structure is what shows us where we should begin to look for our central images and ambiguities.

The difficulty in transferring explication from the reading process to the study of structure has left some curious traces in new critical theory. One of them is in Ransom, with his arbitrary assumption that texture is somehow more important for the critic than structure; another is again in McLuhan, who has expanded the two unresolved factors of explication into a portentous historical contrast between the "linear" demands of the old printed media and the "simultaneous" impact of the new electronic ones. The real distinction however is not between different kinds of media, but between the two operations of the mind which are employed in every contact with every medium. There is a "simultaneous" response to print; there is a "linear" response to a painting, for there is a preliminary dance of the eye before we take in the whole picture; music, at the opposite end of experience, has its score, the spatial presentation symbolizing a simultaneous understanding of it. In reading a newspaper there are two preliminary linear operations, the glance over the headlines and the following down of a story.

This point is crucial for critical theory, because the whole prose-paraphrase conception of "literal" meaning is based on an understanding which is really pre-critical. It is while we are striving to take in what is being presented to us that we are reducing the poetic to the intentional meaning, attending to what the work explicitly says rather than to what it is. The pre-critical experience of literature is wordless, and all criticism which attempts to ground itself on such experience tends to assume that the primary critical act is a wordless reaction, to be described in some metaphor of immediate and non-verbal contact, such as "taste." Verbal criticism, in this view, is a secondary operation of trying to find words to describe the taste. Students who have been encouraged to think along these lines often ask me why I pay so little attention to the "uniqueness" of a work of literature. It may be absurd that "unique" should become a value-term, the world's worst poem being obviously as unique as any other, but the word brings out the underlying confusion of thought very clearly. Criticism is a structure of knowledge, and the unique as such is unknowable; uniqueness is a quality of experience, not of knowledge, and of precisely the aspect of experience which cannot form part of a structure of knowledge.

A better word, such as "individuality," would raise deeper problems. The basis of critical knowledge is the direct experience of literature, certainly, but experience as such is never adequate. We are always reading *Paradise Lost* with a hangover or seeing *King Lear* with an incompetent Cordelia or disliking a novel because some scene in it connects with something suppressed in our memories, and our most deeply satisfying responses are often made in childhood, to be seen later as immature over-reacting. The right occasion, the right mood, the right state of development to meet the occasion, can hardly coincide more than once or twice in a lifetime. Nevertheless, the conception of a definitive experience in time seems to be the *hypothesis* on which criticism is based. Criticism, surely, is designed to reconstruct the kind of experience that we could and should have had, and thereby to bring us into line with that experience, even if the "shadow" of Eliot's *The Hollow Men* has forever darkened it. As a structure of knowledge, then, criticism, like other structures of knowledge, is in one sense a monument to a failure of experience, a tower of Babel or one of the "ruins of time" which, in Blake's phrase, "build mansions in eternity." Hence the popularity of the evaluative or taste-criticism which seems to point backwards to a greater intensity of response than the criticism itself can convey. It corresponds to a popular view of poetry itself, that whatever the poet writes down is merely salvaged from an original "inspiration" of a much more numinous kind. There is a real truth here, though it needs to be differently stated.

There are two categories of response to literature, which could be well described by Schiller's terms naive and sentimental, if used in his sense but transferred from qualities inherent in literature to qualities in the experience of it. The "naive" experience is the one we are now discussing, the linear, participating, pre-critical response which is thrown forward to the conclusion of the work as the reader turns pages or the theatre audience expectantly listens. The conclusion is not simply the last page or spoken line, but the "recognition" which, in a work of fiction particularly, brings the end into line with the beginning and pulls the straight line of response around into a parabola. A pure, self-contained pleasure of participating response is the end at which all writers aim who think of themselves as primarily entertainers, and some of them ignore, resist, or resent the critical operation that follows it.

Such pleasure is however a state of innocence rarely attained in adult life. Many of us have "favorite" authors who set up for us a kind of enclosed garden in which we can wander in a state of completely satisfied receptivity. But for each reader there are very few of these, and they are usually discovered and read fairly early. The sense of guilt about reading "escape" literature is a moral anxiety mainly derived from a feeling that it is a substitute for an unattained experience, and that if escape literature really did what it professes to do it would not be escape literature. As a rule our pleasure in direct response is of a more muted and disseminated kind. It arises from a *habit* of reading or theatre-going, and much of this pleasure comes from a greatly enlarged kind of expectation, extending over many works and many years. Instead of trying to operate the gambling machine of an ideal experience, which may never pay off, we are building something up, accumulating a total fund of experience, each individual response being an investment in it.

It is a central function of criticism to explain what is going on in the habit of reading, using "reading" as a general term for all literary experience. If reading formed simply an unconnected series of experiences, one novel or poem or play after another, it would have the sense of distraction or idle time-filling about it which so many of those who are afraid of leisure believe it to have. The real reader knows better: he knows that he is entering into a coherent structure of experience, and the criticism which studies literature through its organizing patterns of convention, genre and archetype enables him to see what that structure is. Such criticism can hardly injure the "uniqueness" of each experience: on the contrary, it rejects the evaluating hierarchy that limits us to the evaluator's reading list, and encourages each reader to accept no substitutes in his search for infinite variety. It is simply not true that the "great" writers supply all the varieties of experience offered by the merely "good" ones: if Massinger is not a substitute for Shakespeare, neither is Shakespeare a substitute for Massinger.

Still less does the study of the recurring structural patterns of literature lead the reader to the conviction that literature is everywhere much alike. For such study, as just said, does not keep bringing the student back to similar points, but to the same point, to the sense of an identity in literary experience which is the objective counterpart to his own identity. That variety and novelty can be found only at the place of identity is the theme of much of the most influential writing in our century, of the Eliot Quartets with their garlic and sapphires clotting a bedded axle-tree, of the Pound Cantoes which insist on "making it new" but remain at the center of the "unwobbling pivot," of that tremendous hymn to the eternal newness of the same which is *Finnegans Wake.* Twentieth-century criticism which does not understand a central theme of the literature of its own time can hardly be expected to make much sense of the literature of the past.

This brings us to the "sentimental" type of response, which starts where criticism starts, with the unity of the work being read. In modern literature there has been a strong emphasis on demanding a response from the reader which minimizes everything "naive," everything connected with suspense or expectation. This emphasis begins in English literature with the Blake Prophecies, *Milton* and *Jerusalem* particularly, which avoid the sense of linear narration and keep repeating the central theme in an expanding series of contexts. Fiction tends increasingly to abolish the teleological plot which keeps the reader wondering "how it turns out"; poetry drops its connective tissue of narrative in favor of discontinuous episodes; in Mallarmé and elsewhere it even avoids the centrifugal movement of naming or pointing to objects thought of as external to the poem. The emphasis, though it starts with unity, is not on unity for its own sake, but on intensity, a word which brings us back to the conception of an ideal experience. Hopkins with his "inscape" and "instress," Proust with his instants of remembrance and recognition, Eliot with his timeless moments at the world's axis, and a host of more recent writers with their mystiques of orgasm, drugs, and quasi-Buddhist moments of enlightenment, are all talking about a form of ideal experience, which in one way or another seems to be the real goal of life. The ideal experience itself, for the shrewder of these writers at least, never occurs, but with intense practice and concentration a deeply satisfying approximation may occur very rarely. The curious link with religion—for even writers who are not religious still often employ religious terminology or symbolism in this connexion, as Joyce and Proust do—indicates that this direct analogy of ideal experience is typically the way of the mystic or saint rather than the artist—"an occupation for the saint," as Eliot calls it, though he immediately adds that it cannot be in any sense an occupation.

Traditional Christian thought had an explanation for the dilemma of experience which at least made sense within its own postulates. According to it, Adam was capable of a preternatural power of experience before his fall, and we have lost this capacity. Our structures of reason and imagination are therefore analogical constructs designed to recapture, within the mental processes that belong to our present state, something of a lost directness of apprehension. Thus Milton can define education as "an attempt to repair the ruin of our first parents by regaining to know God aright." Similar language continues in our day. Proust concludes his colossal analysis of experience by saying that the only paradises are lost paradises; Yeats, in a much more light-hearted way, tells us in "Solomon and the Witch," anticipating the more recent orgasm cults, that a single act of perfect intercourse would restore the unfallen world. In this view, literature, philosophy and religion at least are all articulate analogies of an experience that goes not only beyond articulateness, but beyond human capacity as well.

The Christian fallen world is only one form of a conception which has run through human imagination and thought from earliest times to the present, according to which the existing world is, so to speak, the lower level of being or reality. Above it is a world which may not exist (we do not actually know that it exists even if we seem to have an experience of it), but is not nothing or non-existence; is not a merely ideal world, because it can act as an informing principle of existence, and yet cannot convincingly be assigned to any intermediate category of existence, such as the potential. This world, related by analogy to the intelligible world of the philosopher and scientist, the imaginable world of the poet, and the revealed world of religion, is increasingly referred to in our day by the term "model." In religion, as noted, this model world is usually projected as an actually existing world created by God, though at present out of human reach. In philosophy it appears in such concepts as Aristotle's final cause, and in the more uninhibited structures of the poets it is the idealized world of romance, pastoral, or apocalyptic vision. As such it suggests a world with which we should wish to identify ourselves, or something in ourselves, and so it becomes the world indicated by the analogy of ideal experience just mentioned.

A direct experience or apprehension of such a world would be a microcosmic experience, an intelligence or imagination finding itself at the centre of an intelligible or imaginable totality, and so experiencing, for however brief an instant, without any residue of alienation. It would thus also be an experience of finally attained or recovered identity. Most of us, at least, never reach it directly in experience, if it is attainable in experience at all, but only through one of the articulated analogies, of which literature is a central one. Whatever it is, it represents the end of our critical path, though we have not as yet traversed the path.

As we proceed to do this, we must keep to a middle way between two uncritical extremes. One is the centrifugal fallacy of determinism, the feeling that literature lacks a social reference unless its structure is ignored and its content associated with something non-literary. No theory is any good unless it explains facts, but theory and facts have to be in the same plane. Psychological and political theories can explain only psychological and political facts; no literary facts can be explained by anything except a literary theory. I remember a student, interested in the Victorian period, who dismissed several standard critical works in that area as "totally lacking in any sense of social awareness." I eventually learned that social awareness, for him, meant the amount of space given in the book, whatever the announced subject, to the Chartist movement. Chartism and similar social movements have their relevance to literature, certainly; but literature is all about something else, even when social protest is its explicit theme.

The other extreme is the centripetal fallacy, where we fail to separate criticism from the pre-critical direct experience of literature. This leads to an evaluating criticism which imposes the critic's own values, derived from the prejudices and anxieties of his own time, on the whole literature of the past. Criticism, like religion, is one of the sub-academic areas in which a large number of people are still free to indulge their anxieties instead of studying their subject. Any mention of this fact is apt to provoke the response: "Of course you don't understand how important our anxieties are." I understand it sufficiently to have devoted a good deal of this essay to the subject of social anxiety and its relation to genuine criticism. We notice that the two fallacies mentioned above turn out to be essentially the same fallacy, as opposed extremes so often do.

Two

The conventions, genres and archetypes of literature do not simply appear: they must develop historically from origins, or perhaps from a common origin. In pursuing this line of thought, I have turned repeatedly to Vico, one of the very few thinkers to understand anything of the historical role of the poetic impulse in civilization as a whole. Vico describes how a society, in its earliest phase, sets up a framework of mythology, out of which all its verbal culture grows, including its literature. Vico's main interest is in the history of law, but it is not difficult to apply his principles to other disciplines.

Early verbal culture consists of, among other things, a group of stories. Some of these stories, as time goes on, take on a central and canonical importance: they are believed to have really happened, or else to explain or recount something that is centrally important for a society's history, religion, or social structure. These canonical stories are, or become, what Vico calls "true fables or myths." Myths are similar in literary form to folk tales and legends, but they have a different social function. They instruct as well as amuse, and sometimes a group of them become esoteric stories, to be revealed only to initiates. Of course any given society may be quite unconscious of any such distinction, but retrospectively we can see how the specific social function or situation of a myth sets it apart from other kinds of story. In the first place, myths stick together to form a mythology, whereas folk tales simply interchange themes and motifs. Thus folk tales can hardly develop characters much beyond the most skeletal types of trickster and ogre and clever riddle-guesser and the like, whereas myths produce gods or cultic heroes who have some permanence, along with a personality distinctive enough to have statues made of them and hymns addressed to them. The story of Odysseus and Polyphemus is not different in literary structure from a folk tale, but it belongs to the group of stories told about Odysseus that make him a recognizable member of a literary family. And because the story is in Homer, it becomes ancestral, the form of the tale that later writers turn to first.

Hence myths not only make up a larger body of mythology, but strike their roots into a specific culture, developing what Ezra Pound, following Frobenius, calls a paideuma. The distinction between myth and folk tale is thus a fateful one for the critic, because the whole historical dimension of literature is bound up with it. Folk tales lead a nomadic literary existence, travelling over the world and passing easily through every barrier of language and custom. If we were to attend only to the similarity in form between myth and folk tale, our approach to literature could not get beyond a facile structuralism. But when a mythology crystallizes in the centre of a culture, a *temenos* or magic circle is drawn around that culture, and a literature develops historically within a limited orbit of language, reference, allusion, belief, transmitted and shared tradition.

In this book we are dealing primarily with the literary aspects of mythology, but as a culture develops, its mythology tends to become encyclopaedic, expanding into a total myth covering a society's view of its past, present and future, its relation to its gods and its neighbours, its traditions, its social and religious duties, and its ultimate destiny. We naturally think of a mythology as a human cultural product, but few societies think of their mythologies at the beginning as something that they have themselves created. They think of them rather as a revelation given them from the gods, or their ancestors, or a period before time began. It is particularly law and religious ritual that are most frequently thought of as divinely revealed. A fully developed or encyclopaedic myth comprises everything that it most concerns its society to know, and I shall therefore speak of it as a mythology of concern, or more briefly as a myth of concern.

The myth of concern exists to hold society together, so far as words can help to do this. For it, truth and reality are not directly connected with reasoning or evidence, but are socially established. What is true, for concern, is what society does and believes in response to authority, and a belief, so far as a belief is verbalized, is a statement of willingness to participate in a myth of concern. The typical language of concern therefore tends to become the language of belief. In origin, a myth of concern is largely undifferentiated: it has its roots in religion, but religion has also at that stage the function of *religio*, the binding together of the community in common acts and assumptions. Later, a myth of concern develops different social, political, legal, and literary branches, and at this stage religion becomes more exclusively the myth of what Tillich calls ultimate concern, the myth of man's relation to other worlds, other beings, other lives, other dimensions of time and space. For a long time this "ultimate" aspect of religion remains in the centre of the total myth of concern. The myth of concern which European and American culture has inherited is, of course, the Judaeo-Christian myth as set out in the Bible, and as taught in the form of doctrine by the Christian Church. The encyclopaedic form of the Bible, stretching from creation to apocalypse, makes it particularly well fitted to provide a mythical framework for a culture, and the form itself illustrates the encyclopaedic inner drive of all developed mythologies.

Concern, so far as it is a feeling, is very close to anxiety, especially when threatened. The anxiety of coherence is central: normally, voices of doubt or dissent are to be muted at all times, and silenced altogether if there is real danger, as in a war. Of almost equal importance is the anxiety of continuity. Religions are deeply conservative in their ritual and in at least the verbal expression of their beliefs; and the etymology of the word superstition associates it with what persists out of mechanical habit. The influence of social concern on literature is to make it intensely traditional, repeating the legends and learning which have most to do with that concern, and which are as a rule well known to the poet's audience. The poet before such an audience is not permitted to depart from the received tradition. We can see this anxiety recurring, phylogenetically, so to speak, in children, with their demands for the invariable repetition of nursery rhymes and tales.

Wisdom, in origin, is the tried and tested way, the way of the elders—for wherever there is anxiety of continuity, parental authority, and the authority of seniors in general, is taken for granted as essential to social security. The archetype of the father handing on the wisdom of his generation to his son, in the form of proverbs or maxims of conduct, has run through literature from the wisdom books of the Old Testament (themselves based on Egyptian and Mesopotamian models which are many centuries older) to Polonius haranguing Laertes and

Lord Chesterfield instructing his heir in a way of life that according to Samuel Johnson combined the morals of a whore with the manners of a dancing-master. In stories based on this archetype (such as the story of Ahikar, which has left its traces in the Apocrypha, the New Testament, the fables of Aesop and the Koran), the son is frequently ungrateful, scatter-brained, or determined to do his own thing. This assimilates the archetype to an even larger and more significant pattern. Before time began, many mythologies tell us, the right way of life, in a body of laws, doctrines or ritual duties, was given by gods or ancestors to their wilful and disobedient children, who forgot or corrupted it. All disaster and bad luck follows from departing from that way, all prosperity from returning to it.

Vico was also the first, so far as I know, to indicate something of the crucial importance of a distinction which has been vigorously pursued by some scholars quite recently. This is the distinction between the oral or pre-literate culture in which the myth of concern normally begins, and the writing culture which succeeds it. It is true that Vico assigns a written language to all three of his historical ages, but the differences among these forms of language, and his insistence that laws can exist independently of writing, give a very different perspective to his argument. An oral culture depends on memory, and consequently it also depends heavily on verse, the simplest and most memorable way of conventionalizing the rhythm of speech. In oral culture mythology and literature are almost coterminous: the chief transmitters of the myth are poets, or people with skills akin to the poetic, who survive in legend or history as bards, prophets, religious teachers, or culture-heroes of various kinds.

Thus in an oral society the poet is a teacher, because he is a man who knows. That is, he is a man who remembers, and who consequently knows the traditional and proper formulas of knowledge. He knows the names of the gods, their genealogy, and their dealings with men; the names of the kings and the tribal legends, the stories of battles won and enemies conquered, the popular wisdom of proverbs and the esoteric wisdom of oracles, the calendar and the seasons, the lucky and unlucky days and the phases of the moon, charms and spells, the right methods of sacrifice, appropriate prayers, and formulas for greeting strangers. In short, he knows the kind of thing that lies behind the poetry of Homer and Hesiod and the heroic poetry of the North, and survives in the popular ballads and folk epics of Slavic countries and Central Asia. I am speaking particularly of the professional oral poet; there are of course other kinds.

The characteristics of oral poetry are familiar, the most familiar being the formulaic unit, the stock epithets and the metrical phrases that can be moved around at will in a poetic process which is always close to improvisation. Such poetry has strong affinities with magic. There is magic in the great roll-calls of names, like the Greek ships in Homer or the elemental spirits in Hesiod, in the carefully stereotyped descriptions of ritual and councils of war, in the oblique and riddling epithets like the Teutonic kenning, in the sententious reflexions that express the inevitable reactions to certain recurring human situations. Magic means secret wisdom, the keys to all knowledge, as becomes more obvious when the poet's repertory of legend expands into an interlocking epic cycle, which begins in turn to suggest the outlines of an encyclopaedic myth of concern. The ideal of universal knowledge achieved in and through poetry has haunted poets and their students from the beginning.

Oral formulaic poetry has a driving power behind it that is very hard to recapture in individually conceived and written poetry. The sinewy strength of Homer is the despair of imitators and translators alike: the style is neither lofty nor familiar, neither naive nor ingenious, but passes beyond all such distinctions. We can get a clearer idea of the effect of such poetry, perhaps, from another formulaic art, the music of the high Baroque. In an intensely formulaic composer, such as Vivaldi, the same scale and chord passages, the same harmonic and melodic progressions, the same cadences, appear over and over again, yet the effect is not monotony but the release of a self-propelled energy. One of the keenest sources of pleasure in listening to poetry or music is the fulfilling of a *general* expectation, of a sort that is possible only in highly conventionalized art. If a particular expectation is being fulfilled, when we know exactly what is going to be said, as in listening to something very familiar, our attention is relaxed, and what we are participating in tends to become either a ritual or a bore, or possibly both. If we have no idea what is coming next, our attention is tense and subject to fatigue. The intermediate area, where we do not know what Pope will say but do know that he will say it in a beautifully turned couplet, where we do not know in a detective story who murdered X but do know that somebody did, is the area of closest unity between poet and audience.

So far as it is a technique, Homer's energy can be matched by the later poets of a writing culture, but the kind of general expectation he raises is based on something that hardly can be. This is the total empathy between poet and audience which arises when the poet is not so much a teacher of his audience or a spokesman for them, as both at once. Such a poet needs to make no moral judgments, for the standards implied are already shared. We cannot even call him a conservative, for that is still a partisan term, and in every judgment or reflective statement he does make he is formulating his hearer's thought as well as his own.

In general, it may be said that oral verbal culture expresses itself in continuous verse and discontinuous prose. Continuous prose is based, not on the physical pulsation of verse, but on a conceptual or semantic rhythm which is much more difficult and sophisticated, and develops later in time. The prose of an oral period, which I shall call the prose of concern, normally takes the form of a discontinuous sequence of easily remembered statements. This type of prose, which is of course written but shows a clear line of oral descent, may be easily illustrated from the Bible and from the fragments of pre-Socratic philosophers. We can isolate certain genres of oral prose, which are the kernels, so to speak, of later prose developments, though in their original form it is often difficult to distinguish prose and verse rhythms.

The kernel of law is the commandment, the prescribed ritual or moral observance; the kernel of philosophy is the aphorism, which has several different social contexts. One is that of the proverb. The proverb is typically the expression of *popular* wisdom: it is generally addressed to those who are without exceptional advantages of birth or wealth, and it is much preoccupied with prudence and caution, with avoiding extremes, with knowing one's place, with being respectful to superiors and courteous to inferiors. The ambiguous oracle and the dark sayings of the wise are more esoteric forms of aphorism. Of more purely literary potential are the parable and the fable, and the later developments of the riddle. The brief anecdote in the life of a teacher which is called a pericope, a set-up situation leading as quickly as possible to some crucial statement or incident, such as a healing, is very conspicuous in the Gospels, which are written throughout in the discontinuous prose of concern. The effect of discontinuity is to suggest that the statements are existential, and have to be absorbed into the consciousness one at a time, instead of being linked with each other by argument. Oracular prose writers from Heraclitus to McLuhan have exploited the sense of extra profundity that comes from leaving more time and space and less sequential connexion at the end of a sentence. The discontinuity of the Essays of Bacon, for example, where (at least in the earliest ones) each sentence is really a paragraph in itself, is connected with his design to "come home to men's business and bosoms," as he put it.

A writing culture reverses the development of oral culture, as its tendency is toward continuous prose and discontinuous verse. This last takes a very long time to manifest itself, poets being a conservative breed inclined to imitate their predecessors, and many centuries of development lie behind the brief lyrics, with the strong visual focus that writing provides, which we find in the Greek Anthology, in Chinese and Japanese poetry, and in French literature of the *symboliste* period. Much earlier, the antithetical patterns of Hebrew parallelism, the Latin elegiac, the English heroic couplet, show the influence of writing in arresting a continuous rhythm and making it return on itself, with the sense of covering a second dimension in space, up and down a page. More immediate, however, is the fact that writing enables continuous prose to develop. Continuous prose means the development of philosophy into a mode of thought articulated by logic and dialectic, and of history into a continuous narrative of events. Such ideas as knowledge for its own sake, or Aristotle's axiom that all men by nature desire to know, are conceptions depending on the existence of written documents, and the metaphor in the phrase "the pursuit of truth (or knowledge) wherever it may lead" shows how closely the sense of knowledge and of the continuous prose made possible by writing are interconnected. Writing also has obviously a central role to play in shifting the main language of concern from the language of prescription, as in the commandment (thou shalt; this do in remembrance of me, etc.), or of myth, as in the story that accounts for the origin of something, into the conceptual and propositional language of belief.

The mental habits brought in by a writing culture thus make a considerable modification in concern. The driving forces binding society together have relaxed somewhat, and man may think of himself, not only as forming part of a community, but also as confronting an objective world or order of nature. In heroic poetry particularly we see how intensely preoccupying is the anxiety of social coherence: the worst and most despicable of vices are those that tend to break down the community of concern, such as treachery or cowardice. In tragedy, where there is a marked tendency to archaism and the use of traditional and primitive settings, characters are defined by their social function, and tragedy itself often turns on the isolating of a central character from his society. Such isolation, whether brought about through external forces or through the unexpected consequences of an act, normally leads to the dissolving of identity, as in the tragedies of Timon and Lear. Whenever a central tragic figure voluntarily isolates himself, like Shakespeare's Richard III with his "I am myself alone," we may be sure that he is up to no good.

But what is terrifyingly abnormal in tragedy is quite normal for a philosopher. From Descartes at least it has been a convention for the philosopher to approach certain problems, such as those of epistemology, in the theoretical isolation of a "subject." He pretends to be alone, cut off from all social preconceptions, and the convention is so well established that it comes as something of a shock to realize that one cannot be without such preconceptions. It is clear that another approach to truth and reality is being made here, and one that tends to individualize a culture. In this context, truth becomes truth of correspondence, the alignment of a structure of words or numbers with a body of external phenomena. I say numbers, because in a writing culture the number also becomes a visual image, hence a writing culture is a counting and measuring culture as well, and scientific and mathematical procedures form part of the change in the mental attitude. We are told that early buildings, including Stonehenge and the Egyptian pyramids, embody precise and complex astronomical observations. But a building, at least one requiring so immense an organization of labour, is the most socially concerned response that it is possible to make to the order of nature. It is not socially disinterested response, any more than the American moon landings of 1969 were disinterested astronomy. "Disinterested" is of course a relative term, never an absolute one, but the relative degrees of it are of great social importance.

The normal tendency of the truth of correspondence is non-mythical, appealing not directly to concern but to more self-validating criteria, such as logicality of argument or (usually a later stage) impersonal evidence and verification. The mental attitudes it develops, however, which include objectivity, suspension of judgment, tolerance, and respect for the individual, become social attitudes as well, and consolidate around a central relationship to society. The verbal expression of concern for these attitudes I shall call the myth of freedom. The myth of freedom is part of the myth of concern, but is a part that stresses the importance of the non-mythical elements in culture, of the truths and realities that are studied rather than created, provided by nature rather than by a social vision. It thus extends to the safeguarding of certain social values not directly connected with the myth of concern, such as the tolerance of opinion which dissents from it.

Concern by itself (so far as we can consider it by itself) has great difficulty in separating appearance from reality. When there is so strong an emphasis on coherence and continuity, what one is and what one does are much the same thing, and similarly society as a whole is essentially what it does. Concern is deeply attached to ritual, to coronations, weddings, funerals, parades, demonstrations, where something is publicly done that expresses an inner social identity. The socially critical attitudes, which perceive hypocrisy, corruption, failure to meet standards, gaps between the real and the ideal, and the like, are anti-ritualistic, and cannot attract much social notice without the support of their one powerful ally, the truth of correspondence revealed through reason and evidence. The myth of freedom thus constitutes the "liberal" element in society, as the myth of concern constitutes the conservative one, and those who hold it are unlikely to form a much larger group than a critical, and usually an educated, minority. To form the community as a whole is not the function of the myth of freedom: it has to find its place in, and come to terms with, the society of which it forms part. Its relation to that society is symbiotic, though sometimes regarded, in times of deep conflict, as simply parasitic.

In oral cultures verbal continuity is preserved mainly in the purely linear form of remembering and passing on. Writing breaks into this temporal movement by providing a visual and spatial focus for a community. In that visual focus there is the source of a greater stability, so that the anxiety of continuity is no longer dependent wholly on memory. According to Socrates in the *Phaedrus*, the Egyptian god Thoth, having invented writing, boasted that his invention would immensely improve the memory, but was told by the other gods that on the contrary it would destroy the memory. The deadlock between a technological expert's enthusiasm and the conservatism of his public has never been more incisively described. Thoth and his critics were talking about different kinds of memory: writing does greatly reduce the social importance of one kind, but it creates another kind of memory, based on a document or physical object which can be compared with other objects. To the extent that the skill of reading and writing spreads, the document acts, potentially, as a *democratizing* force in society by providing an accessible source as a check on tradition, though other social forces, general illiteracy, rare hand-copied manuscripts, censorship, may delay such a development for centuries. In the oral tradition there is a persistent bias toward the esoteric.

In the ancient world, Greek culture made the transition to the mental habits of writing, as far as its minority of cultural leaders was concerned, with fair completeness. The expulsion of poets from Plato's republic was the sign that Greek culture was no longer to be confined by the idioms of the poets. The result for us has been that our whole liberal tradition in education, as the etymology of the word "academic" shows, comes mainly from the Greeks, and our scientific, philosophical, mathematical and historical presuppositions are essentially of Greek origin. A parallel shift to writing and prose took place in Hebrew culture around the time of the Deuteronomic reform, which transformed a mass of legends and oracles into a sacred book written mainly in prose. But the Old Testament maintains a much closer link with the oral tradition and the prose of concern. Philosophy, within the Biblical canon, still retains the form of proverb and oracle: Biblical history is at no time clearly separable from legend or historical reminiscence. This link with oral tradition is still there in Talmudic times, and whatever secular Hebrew or Jewish culture developed did so outside the canon and its commentary. The specific contribution of Hebrew and Biblical mythology to our own culture was in its concentration on a central myth of concern, and the rigorous subordination of all other cultural factors to it. In Greece, on the other hand, Plato's programme of revising and expurgating Greek mythology was not carried out, hence no definitive Greek mythological canon took shape. Homer is not Scripture in the way that the Bible is, and the stories of the gods, for all his authority, remained within the orbit of oral tradition with its formula of "some men say."

The Judaeo-Christian tradition shows us very clearly how truth and reality are conceived by concern. For Judaism, what is true and real is what God says and does; for Christianity, truth is ultimately truth of personality, specifically the personality of Christ. Within Christianity there has always been a feeling that whatever in one's faith is true owes its truth to being in the Bible, or to being taught by the Church on the basis of the Bible. In the First Epistle of John there is a verse setting forth the doctrine of the Trinity which New Testament scholars generally recognize to be a late insertion. The insertion is not simply a pious fraud: if one believes the doctrine of the Trinity, then, from the point of view of the myth of concern, the way to make it true is to get it into the Bible. Nor is the procedure any different from what had gone on in the holy book for centuries: we cannot trace any part of the Bible back to a time when it was not being edited, redacted, conflated, glossed, and expurgated.

When we ask what impelled Hebrew culture to develop its unique conception of a definitive sacred book, one of the answers clearly has to do with the fact that Israel was a defeated and subjected nation, with few intervals of military success and a long memory for them. Monotheism is an idea that would be most naturally suggested by the conception of a world empire. Just as a warrior aristocracy produces an aristocracy of gods, who are assigned to different departments on the analogy of administration, so the conception of a single ruling god seems the appropriate theology for a dominant world state. The first monotheist on record was an Egyptian Pharaoh, and among the most devout monotheists of the ancient world were the world-conquering Persians. The monotheism of the Hebrews, by contrast, was bound up with the dream of achieving some more satisfactory world order in the future. The one God was their God, united in a contract with them, whose will would eventually re-establish their kingdom and overthrow the great empires of the earth. The Jewish conception of a "Day of Jehovah," which was adopted into Christianity as the Last Judgment, points to something very different from imperial monotheism. Hebrew monotheism differed from similar creeds in being a socially and politically revolutionary belief, and this revolutionary quality was inherited by Christianity.

It is hard to overstate the importance for today of the fact that the Western myth of concern is in its origin a revolutionary myth. It amounts to the discovery of a whole new dimension of social time, the sense of a distanced future, as distinct from the pragmatic future revealed by oracle or divination, which is concerned mainly with inquiries about the immediate fortunes of some project, or, at most, about the inquirer's individual fate. Many such discoveries are made easier, or even possible, by something suggesting them in the grammar of a language, such as a verb-tense system which includes a future: the absence of this in the Hebrew language indicates how powerful was the social energy behind the discovery. The same culture, for the same reasons, produced the conception of the *apocryphon*, the book which is to be sealed up in its own time and opened when its time has come, which underlies a good deal of the psychology of creation in Western literature, especially in the last two or three centuries.

The reaction to early Christianity was typical of conservative reactions to revolutionary movements. The earliest external reference to Christians, in Tacitus' *Annals*, speaks of them with a blistering contempt which is highly significant, coming as it does from a by no means weak or hysterical writer. Much later, the Emperor Marcus Aurelius complained that he had tried to get rid of the Christians by persecution, but had been unable to make much impression on them because of their *parataxis,* their military discipline. Even he did not recognize that the Christian Church had been duplicating the Roman authority with a power-structure which could go underground in time of persecution until the time came for it to emerge and take over. Eventually that time came, and then, of course, the cyclical movement which is inherent in the very word "revolution" began to operate.

In every structured society the ascendant class attempts to take over the myth of concern and make it, or an essential part of it, a rationalization of its ascendancy. In proportion as Christianity gained secular authority, its myth of concern tended to associate itself with the myths of the various ascendant classes as they succeeded one another. In the Middle Ages, the conception of a structure of authority, requiring protection from above and obedience from below, found its way into the religious myth as well as the social system. The connexion between Protestantism and the rise of the bourgeoisie has been considerably over-labored by historians and social scientists, but still in the nineteenth century Matthew Arnold was able, with some plausibility, to associate the "Hebraic" or Judaeo-Christian tradition with the mores of the Victorian middle class. Certainly the association of Christianity with the middle class did a good deal to popularize the Marxist conception of a proletarian or excluded-class myth of concern. Yet Christianity has always remained a revolutionary myth, never completely merging with any ascendant-class myth in the way that, apparently, Hinduism and Confucianism did in the Far East.

This fact gives Christianity a positive vitality in our own

day; it also, however, gave it a negative vitality which eventually began to produce rivals to it. We saw that a religious myth of concern tends increasingly as it goes on to specialize in another world, and by the eighteenth century the growing ineffectiveness of the politically revolutionary element in Christianity, despite such movements as Methodism, brought about a crisis. The Christian monopoly of the Western myth of concern began to give way to a more pluralistic situation in which a number of new and more secular myths shared the field with it. Naturally, there were many who insisted that the true myth of concern could only be found in a revived Christianity, and the production of such manifestoes has been a cultural heavy industry ever since. But not many of these—not even those of Kierkegaard, who was more aware of the kind of implications we have been considering here than most—have been able or willing to recognize the revolutionary element in Christianity as essential to its effectiveness, perhaps even to its validity.

Of the new political myths of concern that began to arise from the eighteenth century on, the most important were the myth of democracy and the revolutionary working-class myth which eventually found its focus in Marxism. The former, which drew from both Classical and Christian sources, was a myth of concern which attempted to incorporate a myth of freedom within itself; the latter was a more direct descendant of the original Judaeo-Christian revolutionary attitude. The link of continuity between Christianity and Marxism is superficially less obvious than the Greek ancestry of our academic and liberal attitudes, because every revolution forms itself in opposite to its predecessor. But the link is there: it is not easy to break out of the mental habits formed by a mythical framework, or what is often called tradition, and even if it is possible we must first know what that tradition is.

There are in particular three characteristics of a revolutionary movement that Christianity and Marxism share. One of these is the belief in a unique historical revelation. This belief, which gives so many liberals so much difficulty with Christianity, is an essential part of a revolutionary mode of thought: a revolution starts then and there, not at various places and times. It begins with Jesus and not with the Pharisees or Essenes; with Marx and not with Owen or the Saint-Simonians. Along with the uniqueness goes the conception of a canon of essential and approved texts, and a clear drawing of lines against even the most neighborly of heresies. In fact, the attack on the heresy helps to define a revolutionary doctrine in a way that an attack on total opposition does not. Christianity defined itself, not by attacking unbelievers, but by attacking Arians or Gnostics and calling them unbelievers; Marxism defines itself, not by attacking capitalist imperialism, but by attacking Trotsky or Liu Shao-Chi and calling them agents of capitalist imperialism. A third characteristic is the resistance to any kind of "revisionism," or incorporating of other cultural elements into the thought of the revolutionary leadership. The revolutions within Christianity, notably the Protestant ones, usually professed to be a return to the pure gospel of their founder, and this must also be the professed aim of new Marxist party lines. There is even an ultra-Puritan movement in Marxism back to the early alienation essays of Marx, before social and institutional Marxism began. The anti-revisionist tendency is normally an anti-liberal tendency. Revolutions, naturally, are directed against a power-holding ascendancy, and liberals, from "enervate Origen," as Eliot calls him, to Erasmus, and from Erasmus to the political liberals of our own day, are regularly taken by revolutionaries to be, consciously or unconsciously, spokesmen for the opposed establishment.

In the earlier Christian centuries, the dethroned "pagan" tradition began slowly to form a liberal opposition, modifying, relaxing, and expanding the revolutionary narrowness of the Christian myth of concern, and so forming the basis of a myth of freedom. Some of this was reflected in literature: we shall return to this later, but may note here the convention of love poetry, developed mainly from Ovid. This made it imaginatively clear that Eros was a mighty force to be reckoned with, in contrast to official Christianity, which, like most revolutionary movements, required from its most dedicated followers the extra energy that comes from sexual sublimation. Again, the Christian myth, by remaining so close to the oral tradition, had thrown a strong emphasis on the ear, on the hearing of the word, on the receptivity to authority that binds a society together. In the word "idolatry," and in its recurring iconoclasm, Christianity expressed its antagonism to the hypnotizing power of the external visible world. It was a more liberal expansion of Christian culture that developed the visual arts, including the arts of the theatre, so much disliked by the more rigorous Christians, including Pascal and many of the Puritans. The growing realism and direct observation of experience and nature in Western art also helped to relax the Christian preoccupation with unifying society in a common bond of belief. The Christian teaching that there were no gods and nothing numinous in nature, that nature was a fellow-creature of man, and that the gods men had previously discovered in nature were all devils, reflects a fear of turning away from social concern to the order of nature. After the turn had become irrevocable, the belief persisted for centuries that the order which the scientist finds in nature could only be accounted for as a product of a divine mind. This assumption has no intellectual function in science; its function is social, an attempt on the part of a dominant myth of concern to contain a restive and struggling myth of freedom.

The central question of concern, what must we do to be

saved? is much the same in all ages, but naturally the conceptions of salvation vary. There are two worlds for man: one is the environment of nature, which is presented to man objectively and must be studied and examined; the other is the civilization that he accepts or tries to modify. For traditional Christianity, God alone is creative, and he created not only the order of nature but the models of human civilization as well. God built the first city and planted the first garden; God was the first artist, nature being the art of God; God designed the primary laws of mankind and revealed to him the true religion. For most myths of concern in our day, and for all radical ones, the only creative power in the situation comes from man himself, hence its truth or reality is connected with human desire, with what we want to see exist, and with human practical skill, with what we are able to make exist. Marx did not, so far as I know, speak of this created reality as myth: that association for revolutionary thought was made later, chiefly by Sorel, though it is implied in Hegel's shift of the absolute from substance to subject which is adopted in Marx's Theses on Feuerbach. When we hear that it is more important to change the world than to study it, we know that there is, once again, a social movement on foot to subordinate all philosophical myths of freedom to a new myth of concern.

The greater myths of concern, the ones that have permanently altered the social consciousness of man, have usually begun in a mood perhaps best called abhorrence. Abhorrence of idolatry, of sin, of exploitation, of what the soul in Yeats calls the crime of death and birth: these are great revulsions that have produced the Jewish law, the Christian church, the Marxist party, the teachings of the compassionate Buddha. The real enemies of such movements are not those who oppose but those who are indifferent: the opposite of faith is not doubt, but the inability to see what all the fuss is about. It is possible that similar moods are growing among us. We tend to associate the physical enemies of society, poverty and disease and filth, mainly with "underdeveloped" nations. But we may also feel that the same words apply equally to our mean streets, our vacuous mass media, our stinking and murderous automobiles. When such feelings are reinforced by more theoretical conceptions like the "profit motive," a myth of concern is developing. In the past, such revulsions, when deep enough, have turned the cycle of history again by forming a new organization that has dominated its culture, sometimes for centuries.

According to Vico, history takes the form of a series of cycles of this kind, starting off with a revulsion, which he symbolizes by the fear of thunder, from a mindless and undirected existence. There comes a stage of development in history, however, at which we feel that we have outgrown certain previous stages that were cruel or superstitious, and all cyclical movements bring with them the dreary humiliation of having to return to these earlier stages. The moment of this return coincides closely with the coming of a new myth of concern to social supremacy. It is an ancient axiom, transmitted by Lucretius, that the social effects of religions, that is, structures of belief and concern generally, are evil in direct proportion to their temporal power and influence. In Christian times there were some thinkers, including the authors of the medieval *Defensor Pacis,* who found temporal authority to be the essential source of corruption in the church. Even yet, whenever a new and powerful myth of concern develops, we can see a dark age, or what Gibbon called the triumph of barbarism and religion, in its penumbra, as soon as it turns from exhortation to organization.

As the "Decline and Fall" of Gibbon's title shows, there is a rhythm of death and rebirth in concern: what declined and fell was perhaps as much a mystique as an actual authority collecting taxes and administering laws. But there is no fatality in such matters, no necessity to go around a circle again, no need to relinquish what we have wrested from bigotry and cruelty. The abhorred world is the other aspect of what we met in the previous section as the model world: in literature it is primarily the world of irony and satire, as the model world is most directly expressed in idyl and pastoral and idealized romance. Like the model world, it is most useful to us when kept before us in the present, both as an imaginative vision and as an enemy to be fought, not projected into the past, as part of a lost-paradise or other alienation myth, or into the future, where escaping from it is associated with some progressive or revolutionary donkey's carrot.

When we look at whatever it is in our own world that makes it not quite the abhorred world, but something we can live with in the meantime, we find that one of the most important elements is the tension between concern and freedom. When a myth of concern has everything its own way, it becomes the most squalid of tyrannies, with no moral principles except those of its own tactics, and a hatred of all human life that escapes from its particular obsessions. When a myth of freedom has everything its own way, it becomes a lazy and selfish parasite on a power-structure. Satire shows us in 1984 the society that has destroyed its freedom, and in *Brave New World* the society that has forgotten its concern. They must both be there, and the genuine individual and the free society can exist only when they are.

Three

In trying to see where literature belongs in this dialectic of concern and freedom, we can, I think, gain a great deal from a renewed study of the two classical "defences" of poetry in English literature by Sidney and Shelley. Both works are familiar, but in the present context they may show less familiar aspects. They come out of the centres of two movements in English culture, Renaissance humanism and Romanticism, which are stages of major importance on our critical path. Defence implies attack: Sidney's essay is usually contrasted with the kind of anti-poetic statement often called "Puritan," such as Gosson's *School of Abuse* (although technically Gosson was less of a Puritan than Sidney), and Shelley takes off from his friend Peacock's satire, *The Four Ages of Poetry*. Attacks on poetry in their turn can tell us a good deal about the social anxieties which work against the poet in every age.

Man lives, we remarked, in two worlds. There is the world he is actually in, the world of nature or his objective environment, and there is the civilization he is trying to build or maintain out of his environment, a world rooted in the conception of art, as the environment is rooted in the conception of nature. For the objective world he develops a logical language of fact, reason, description and verification: for the potentially created world he develops a mythical language of hope, desire, belief, anxiety, polemic, fantasy and construction. This kind of language is always related in some way or other to an ideal form of civilization. For most people today the ideal form is associated with the future, as the world we want to live in; in previous ages it was usually associated with the past or a timeless period before history began.

In its "pure" form, concern is expressed by an unquestioning belief that cares little for evidence or reason, or, at least, does not depend on them. But as the sense of the importance of truth of correspondence makes itself felt, concern must meet and reckon with this other aspect of the mind's sense of reality. Its first attempt to do so is to construct a deductive synthesis of experience, in which the principles of concern form the major premises and the facts of experience are supposed to be logically related to them.

This is the tendency in medieval philosophy which reached its culmination in Thomism. Underlying it was a gigantic effort to show that Christianity possessed the truth of correspondence as well as the truth of revelation, and was true by the tests of reason and historical evidence. Christian faith, or central body of articulated concern, thus became the basis for the deductive rational structure provided by theology, from which in turn principles of philosophy, and eventually science, were, at least ideally, to be deduced. Marxism is still struggling with a similar deductive scholasticism, maintaining that its principles are "scientific," that is, valid major premises of science. In the democracies, too, a strong hankering for an encyclopaedic synthesis of thought, which would have a solidly established body of scientific facts and laws as its foundation and the premises of belief and hope as its superstructure, keeps recurring in every generation. After Hegel's *Phenomenology of the Spirit,* such ambitions gave a strongly cosmological slant to nineteenth-century philosophy, when constructing encyclopaedic "systems," or verbal cathedrals of knowledge and faith, was so often regarded as philosophy's primary task. It may be significant that really thoroughgoing efforts to "reconcile" the two kinds of reality turn out to be cannibalistic ones: in Hegel knowledge ultimately swallows faith, as in the *Summa contra Gentiles* faith ultimately swallows knowledge.

Still, the medieval Christian mythical framework was comprehensive enough to contain what we have called the "liberal opposition" of Classical-based learning and culture—which, of course, was not an opposition in the sense of a different group of people holding a different myth of concern. By the sixteenth century the deductive synthesis, though still there, existed in what Wallace Stevens calls ghostlier demarcations. It had been weakened by the attacks on one of its main supports, the real universal, in nominalist philosophy, and was still further weakened, in England, by the Protestant Reformation, the general tendency of Protestantism being to separate the areas of faith and knowledge. In this situation the "liberal opposition," aided by the spread of higher education among the laity, the invention of the printing press, and the increase of centralized authority in nations and city-states, consolidated into humanism, and took on a central role in Renaissance society.

Humanism may be seen, from our present point of view, as a stage in the accommodation of a society's literary culture to a dominant myth of concern. Historically, it was the inevitable second stage after the breakdown of the effort at deductive synthesis. The humanists were mainly, to use a somewhat worn phrase, "Christian humanists": they would have thought it absurd to try to go back to paganism or polytheism, and to construct a new myth of concern would have destroyed the whole idea of humanism. For all the interest that the humanists took in Biblical and theological scholarship, and for all the broad range of their practical interests, the idea of humanism is of something different from, and complementary to, the religious and political concerns of their age.

For many centuries the mental habits of a writing culture had got sufficiently in the ascendant for the language of prose and reason to be regarded as the primary verbal expression of reality. It was accepted that no poet can be regarded as having, in religion, the kind of authority that the theologian has; and in history and morals too the language of poetry falls short of the language of what is considered literal truth. Once a writing culture has been established, the central oral figure in it becomes the orator. Humanism took over the central conceptions of the oratorical culture of Augustan Rome, including the conception of an encyclopaedic learning acquired through a rhetorical training. The theory of this is set out in Cicero's *De Oratore*, and its presence or assumed presence in Virgil was one of the things that gave him so legendary a reputation in the Middle and later ages.

Augustan culture was contemporary with two other social developments, which for the historical perspective of humanism were definitive: the centralizing of temporal authority in the Emperor and the beginning of Christianity. Naturally the humanists, like their medieval predecessors, assumed the connexions between the infant Empire and the infant Church to be much closer than they were. Virgil's Fourth Eclogue and the "Great Pan is dead" story in Plutarch were assumed to be Messianic prophecies; Seneca was believed to be a correspondent of St. Paul; Ovid's *Metamorphoses* was a kind of pagan

Bible, stretching as it does from creation and flood stories to visions of the end of nature. In Ovid, Virgil, Horace, and elsewhere there are moods haunted by a sense of a fateful change in human affairs, which Yeats expresses in the phrase "Full Moon in March," a phrase linking the murder of Caesar and the Resurrection, and such moods were naturally associated with the birth of Christ by Christian ages. Thus the period of Augustus had something about it of a secular as well as a sacred incarnation.

As such it had a particular significance for a movement which claimed neither the spiritual authority of Christianity nor the temporal power of prince or Emperor, but attempted to establish a kind of elite balancing group in society, enabling the scholarship and culture of that society to develop under the protection of the two authorities. Christianity had the truth, but it did not have style: St. Paul wrote inferior Greek, and patristic Latin was not to be compared to Cicero. The prince had power, and theoretically he was the most important person to be given the encyclopaedic orator's training, hence such treatises as Erasmus' *Institute of a Christian Prince* or Elyot's *The Governour,* for which the great Classical prototype was Xenophon's *Cyropaedia,* the ideal education of the ideal prince. But in practice the prince was more likely to be a man of will, and the humanist's social function, in practice, was closer to that of the servant and adviser of the prince, the courtier whose education is outlined in Castiglione.

In medieval literature we often meet the conception of the chivalric ring, the group of knights united by some circular symbol like the Garter or the Round Table, who are dedicated to the service of the prince and to the social ideals of the Church. The theme of the chivalric ring, which usually dissolves in some tragic or elegiac conclusion, has run through

English literature from the *comitatus* groups in the earliest heroic poetry to Tennyson—in fact to T. H. White and Tolkien. In some respects the humanists formed a civilian and intellectual counterpart to the chivalric ring, and the connexion between them is the theme of the greatest English poem of Renaissance humanism, Spenser's *Faerie Queene.* Here a group of knights go through the regular chivalric routines of rescuing maidens and killing dragons and giants, but all this activity really symbolizes the ideal cultural and religious education of the ideal Christian and Renaissance prince.

The humanist was typically scholar and critic rather than poet, and humanism saw itself as establishing a social framework for the poet as well as suggesting to him the conventions and norms of his expression. Not only were there major and minor poets, there were major and minor genres as well, the major genres, epic in particular, having the particular social role of dealing with ruling-class figures and of requiring from the poet something of the encyclopaedic range of learning that Homer and Virgil were assumed to have possessed before him. This learning was to be derived from the whole body of Classical literature, as well as Christian literature, and for the humanist Greek and Latin authors were authoritative in all branches of learning, Vitruvius in architecture and Galen in medicine no less than Cicero and Virgil in literature. The printing press, by enabling scholars to establish an *editio princeps* and lift a Classical text out of the corrupting stream of time with all its hazards of scribal errors and manuscripts neglected by ignorance, had a central role in dramatizing this sense of authority and intellectual community. Thus it represents a higher stage in the creation of a spatial focus for a community which we have seen to be inherent in all forms of writing.

The literary genres of humanism itself, which were those of

Cicero, and before him of Plato, represent the kind of development of concerned prose that we should expect from its cultural situation. They include the formal epistle, where the writer speaks as one member of a dedicated community to another, the rhetorical defence of which Sidney's apology is an example, the dialogue with a symposium setting, and the educational treatise, sometimes taking the form of a Utopia, in imitation of Plato's *Republic* and the parallel treatise of Cicero from which the *Somnium Scipionis* comes. All of these are genres expressing the sense of the social importance of literary education. Encyclopaedic learning is not specialized learning: versatility is a humanist ideal, because only through versatility can one keep a sense of social perspective, seeing the whole range and scope of a community's culture. As a scholar, the humanist might be specialized to the degree of Browning's grammarian, but, like him, he related his specialization to a comprehensive social vision.

This vision was never far from that of the amateur, who is the courtly ideal of Castiglione, and whose primary social function is to be a patron and connoisseur of the arts. For Castiglione the courtly amateur does everything with an ease and a lightness (*sprezzatura*) that suggests play, which in its turn suggests the social rank of the gentleman, the person freed, not from social responsibility, but from the obligations of labor. The humanist tended to distrust technical language, of the kind that cannot be digested into cultivated conversation, because it suggested the laborious or professional activities of a lower social rank. This prejudice was carried to the point of making the name of the great analytical genius Duns Scotus, with his technical philosophical vocabulary, into a synonym of stupidity. The humanist's training was rhetorical, and rhetoric had developed a formidable jargon of its own, but nevertheless gentlemen do not use "inkhorn terms" in their conversation or writing. This social attitude is reflected in the fact that the great philosophers of the next two centuries were, in the strict sense, amateurs, unconnected with the profession of the "schoolmen."

"Ye know not," said Roger Ascham, "what hurt ye do to learning, that care not for words, but for matter, and so make a divorce betwixt the tongue and the heart. For mark all ages . . . and ye shall surely find that, when apt and good words began to be neglected . . . then also began ill deeds to spring, strange manners to oppress good orders, new and fond opinions to strive with old and true doctrine, first in Philosophy, and after in Religion." We notice the strength of what we have called the anxiety of continuity in this passage, which is typical of humanism; but the same *topos* is being repeated in the next century by Milton in a more revolutionary context: "For let the words of a country be in part unhandsome and offensive in themselves, in part debased by wear and wrongly uttered, and what do they declare but, by no light indication, that the inhabitants of that country are an indolent, idly-yawning race, with minds already long prepared for any amount of servility? On the other hand, we have never heard that any empire, any state, did not flourish moderately at least as long as liking and care for its own language lasted."

Ascham indicates how humanism thought of itself as providing the complement to social authority. Real authority comes from church and state, who implement the spiritual and secular forms of what we have been calling the myth of concern. Precise, disciplined, elegant speech is the manifestation, or audible presence, of this order and stability in society. The order of the community and the order of communication are connected, not magically, but as reality and appearance. Humanism was not scientific nor particularly sympathetic to the new science:

it was a cult of authority, precisely because it was a literary movement, revolving around its classics rather than developing and advancing in time, as science does. And yet, as we see in Milton, this deeply conservative attitude of humanism, its devotion to order and discipline, is not necessarily a part of an authoritarian view of society. Humanism provides a social situation for the poet in a writing and reasoning culture in which the poet, like Cressida, deserts the defending camp for the besieging one. That is, instead of being the teacher of the myth of concern, he becomes a part of the myth of freedom, deeply indebted to Classical culture, which he uses as a kind of liberal and imaginative counterpoint against a Christian theme. He has, of course, little connection with anything that we put at the basis of the myth of freedom, the non-mythical elements of logic, evidence and verification that underlie philosophy and the sciences. He does, however, represent something of the spirit of "ancient liberty" that Milton always associates with Classical literature in its best periods. In the oratorical tradition there had always been an association with political freedom, beginning with Demosthenes and his struggle against Macedonian imperialism. Even Cicero, for all his political ineptness, carried something of this aura, some of which rubbed off on his very un-oratorical contemporary Cato.

I am setting Sidney's defence in the context of the humanist movement because his view of poetry is so centrally typical of it. As soon as we ask why a defence of poetry should be needed, we are carried into the centre of the humanist situation. Many people in Sidney's day and later were obsessed with the values of a writing culture. Religion for most of them was derived from a book; it was spiritually dangerous to be illiterate, yet the religion had to be understood from the book in the plainest prose terms. Hence the attitude of such pamphleteers as Gosson, who demanded to know why Plato was not right, and why the poets with their outworn modes of thought and their hankering for the fabulous should still have a claim on our attention.

Gosson is something of a straw man in Sidney, if he is there at all, and the sense of social threat is not very oppressive. Nevertheless there is something in Sidney, as in most of his contemporaries, of a feeling that the poet has been dispossessed from a greater heritage. In a distant past, even before Homer, a period associated with such legendary names as Musaeus, Linus and Orpheus, along with Zoroaster in religion and Hermes Trismegistus in philosophy, the poet, we are so often told in Renaissance criticism, was the lawgiver of society, the founder of civilization. This refers, as noted previously, to the social conditions of an oral or pre-literate culture, in which the professional poet is, if not exactly a lawgiver, at least an educator, the man who knows because he remembers.

The encyclopaedic drive in a myth of concern was also sensed by Elizabethan critics as something that was in or immediately behind Homer, and they had the same kind of sentimental admiration for it that many people in our day have had for the cultural synthesis of the Middle Ages—a comparison which, as we have seen, is not a random one. Sidney stresses such themes less than many of his contemporaries— Chapman, for example—but still they are there, attached to the common Renaissance assumption that in all human achievements the greatest are the earliest. The poet is now in a subordinate social role and must come to terms with it, even to the point of writing a defence of poetry. But he can never forget the glamor of his ancient heritage, the days when divine inspiration descended on him with the *raptus* of authentic prophecy. "Est deus in nobis," said Ovid. This "deus" is not a god any more, only a psychological and subjective power, but it is still numinous, still speaks with a mysterious and awful authority, and is still dangerous to trifle with.

The general critical position of Sidney is contained within the same Christian framework of assumptions as that of the detractors of poetry. In a writing culture the norms of meaning are established by the non-literary writers: it is the discursive prose writers who really mean what they say, and align their words accurately with the facts or propositions they are conveying. Compared with them, the poet's meaning is indirect, or ironic, as we should say now. The apologist for poetry has first of all to consider the question: is poetry genuinely educational? For Sidney, as for his contemporaries generally, the aim of education, in the broadest sense, is the reform of the will, which is born in sin and headed the wrong way. Truth, by itself, cannot turn the will, but poetry in alliance with truth, using the vividness and the emotional resonance peculiar to it, may move the feelings to align themselves with the intelligence, and so help to get the will moving. The function of poetry, then, is to provide a *rhetorical analogue* to concerned truth. Rhetoric, said Aristotle, is the *antistrophos,* the answering chorus, of truth, and whatever genuine social function the poet has depends on the consonance between his rhetoric and the rational disciplines, with their more exact relation to reality.

Thus the conception of poetry in Sidney is an application of the general humanist view of disciplined speech as the manifestation or audible presence of social authority. In its relation to secular concern, more particularly to military courage, we discover that poetry is, not a corrupter of courage, but "the companion of camps." In relation to Christian concern, poetry leads us out of the lower level of nature, the ordinary physical world which is essentially alien to man, to the upper level of genuinely human nature, where man ought to be and originally was, the level symbolized in myths of Paradise and a Golden Age. Hence Sidney says that nature's world is brazen, and that only the poets give us a golden one, and also that poetry develops a "second nature" by relating itself to an ideal world where the distinction between art and nature has ceased to exist.

The next question to meet is the one raised by the attack on poetry as dealing only with the untrue or the fabulous. Here Sidney follows the line of argument which had descended from Aristotle, that the truthful statement is the specific and particular statement. There are two kinds of such statements: the historical or factual, and the predicated or conceptual: the former are examples or instances, the latter principles or precepts. Poetry withdraws from particular statements: the poet, Sidney says, never affirms or denies. He produces his own distinctive kind of statement, which combines the example of the historian with the precept of the moral philosopher. As compared with the historian, the poet gives us not the existential but the recurring or essential event; as compared with the moralist, he tells us not the essential but the existential truth, the kind of truth that can only be presented through illustration or parable. What is most distinctive about poetry is the poet's power of illustration, a power which is partly an ability to popularize and make more accessible the truths of revelation and reason.

Here is the reason for the importance, for humanist critics, of the tag *ut pictura poesis*. Poetry is a speaking picture, presenting vividly and without pedantry or jargon what it most concerns us to understand. There is thus no inconsistency in saying, on the one hand, that the poet popularizes the rational disciplines, sugar-coats the pill, provides instruction for the simple, and on the other hand that great poetry is a treasure trove of esoteric wisdom which poets hid in parables "lest by profane wits it should be abused," as Sidney says. Both these views of poetry can be understood through the same axiom of *ut pictura poesis,* which assumes that only the simple and the vivid can be genuinely profound. Pedantry and jargon, the languages of specialized learning, produce obscurity, but the profundity of obscurity is not genuine.

We see from this how the documentary or "background" interests of later criticism have originated. The way to make sense of the study of poetry, in this view, is to relate it to the two neighboring disciplines that make literal statements and actually tell the truth and give the facts. We are back at the theoretical muddle referred to earlier, where we understand a poem "literally" through the kind of meaning which it shares with non-literary writing. The axiom *ut pictura poesis,* however, clearly implies that the poem really means, not what it says, but what it illustrates or shows forth. Sidney himself is not fully conscious of this implication, which is of immense importance for critical theory, but it agrees with the drift of his argument. What the poet says is of limited importance: whatever it is, other forms of verbal expression say it in a way that comes closer to "literal" truth. The poet in Sidney's day was, of course, greatly prized for his capacity to make sententious statements, of the kind that readers and schoolboys copied out in their commonplace books. But the more admirable the sentence, the more it is an echo of what we already know in a different way. Gerard Manley Hopkins draws a distinction between a poet's "overthought" or explicit meaning, and his "underthought," or texture of images and metaphors. But a poet's underthought, his metaphorical or pictured meaning, is clearly his real thought, and in a writing culture it to some degree even separates itself from the explicit statement.

When we look at Shakespeare, we realize that Elizabethan culture is still very largely oral, and that the existence of a popular poetic theatre is evidence of the fact. In Shakespeare we see a good deal of the poet's original oral educating function still going on, most obviously in the histories. Shakespeare also shows the identification with the audience's attitude that the oral poet has. On the level of explicit statement, or what the play appears to be saying, he seems willing to accept the assumption, or implication, that Henry V was a glorious conqueror and Joan of Arc a wicked witch, that Shylock is typical of Jews and Judaism, that peasants are to be seen through the eyes of the gentry, that the recognized sovereign is the Lord's anointed and can cure diseases in virtue of being so, and many other things that the modern critic passes over in embarrassed silence. With Shakespeare we are still many centuries removed from T. S. Eliot's comparison of the explicit meaning of a poem to a piece of meat that a burglar throws to a watchdog to keep him quiet. But there is clearly something in the uncritical postulates of Shakespeare that has to do with soothing popular anxieties and keeping a vigilant and by no means unintelligent censorship from getting stirred up.

I am not of course speaking of a conscious policy on Shakespeare's part: I am merely applying to him a central critical principle. Questionable or dated social attitudes, as expressed in what appears to be the surface meaning, do not affect the real meaning of poetry, which is conveyed through a structure of imagery and action. When we examine the imagery of *Henry V,* and listen carefully to the moods and overtones which that imagery suggests, we realize that the play is very far from expressing the simpleminded patriotism that it appears to be expressing. Of course we do not ignore or set aside the explicit meaning (unless what we are reading happens to be an ironic allegory), but if we give primary importance to the primary meaning, the explicit meaning will take on a very different relation to it.

Two corollaries are important here. One is, that there can be no definitive rendering of the real poetic meaning: it cannot, like the explicit meaning, be grasped in a way that makes it possible for us to say that this is what Shakespeare really meant, or had in mind, or was trying to say, or whatever such silly phrase we use. Grasping the real meaning of poetry gives us an orbit or circumference of meaning, within which there is still some latitude for varieties of interpretation and emphasis, both in commentary and, with a play, in performance. The other relates to the question whether a translation should be literal or faithful merely to the general spirit. This is not an either-or question at all: a translation should be as literal a rendering as possible of the metaphorical structure of the original, as it is in all the best translations of the humanist period, from Wyatt's paraphrases of Petrarch to the 1611 Bible.

Ever since Plato the question has been raised: in what sense does the poet know what he is talking about? The poet seems to have some educational function without being himself necessarily an educator: he knows what he is doing, certainly what he is saying, but *qua* poet can say it only in the form of his poem. After poetic meaning becomes more obviously, with the rise of writing, what is imaged or shown forth rather than what is said, the educational aspect of the poet's function clearly has to be taken over by someone else. In oral days the poet had, for interpreter, only the rhapsode, who, as Socrates demonstrates in the *Ion*, really knows nothing at all; with the coming of more sequential forms of thinking the critic appears as the poet's social complement.

The critic was, from ancient times to the Renaissance, related to an elite community of scholars, orators and intellectuals concerned with words; but it was particularly Renaissance humanism that established the critic as the judge of the poet. From the humanist point of view the critic was in a superior position to the poet, not personally or socially, but as the spokesman for the society which established the norms to which the poet conformed. This society was primarily the humanist elite, but the humanist elite in its turn spoke for and interpreted the norms of society as a whole. When Addison says, in Spectator 29, that the arts "are to deduce their Laws and Rules from the general Sense and Taste of Mankind, and not from Principles of those Arts themselves; or in other Words, the Taste is not to conform to the Art, but the Art to the Taste," he is talking stark nonsense from the modern critic's point of view. But he speaks for a humanistic society that was confident of its standards, believed in a progressive refinement of manners, and felt that it was entitled to represent the general sense and taste of mankind.

In Sidney's day humanism had little interest in science, with its appeal to experience and verification, but in the next century the atmosphere changed. One of the speakers in Dryden's *Essay on Dramatic Poesy* says: "If natural causes be more known now than in the time of Aristotle, because more studied, it follows that poesy and other arts may, with the same pains, arrive still nearer to perfection." This comment indicates a growing rapprochement between humanism and science, when the gentleman amateur had begun to develop an interest in the study of nature. Hence the humanist's preoccupation with Classical literature began to include a more philosophical and scientific spirit as well. The effect of such expanded Classicism on literature was to encourage a cult of good sense, a coherent and articulate literary community, and an assimilation of culture and taste: in short the eighteenth-century culture which we still instinctively call "Augustan." This consolidated Classicism was mainly, except for some of the Deists, still thought of as analogous and complementary to Christianity, and the influence of Newton reinforced this attitude. Later on, in

Shelley and several of the German Romantics, we find the suggestion that the real myth of concern in Western culture is Classical rather than Christian in origin. This suggestion recurs in the restatement of the traditional humanist position in Matthew Arnold's *Culture and Anarchy*. I am writing in the centenary year of that book (1969), and nobody can be writing on such a subject as mine in this year without being aware that the confrontation of culture and anarchy has taken a very different form from the one that Arnold envisaged.

According to Arnold, the "Hebraic" revolutionary myth of concern was losing its impetus, running into the desert sands of bourgeois morality. Other revolutionary movements were beginning to take shape. One was a cult of "doing as one likes", the other a working-class movement that was making ominous noises after the passing of the Second Reform Bill. Both represented anarchy, and the remedy for them was "culture," for Arnold a myth of concern which held the essence of everything good in conservative, liberal and radical values. It was conservative because it was aware of and accepted its tradition, and because it was a source of social authority. It was liberal because it was held, not through faith or dogma, but through reason and imagination, incorporating a sense of beauty and the virtues of the liberal attitude, including tolerance and suspended judgment. Consequently the real source of its tradition was Hellenic rather than Hebraic. It was radical because its authority was ultimately a spiritual authority, and so its long-run influence was an equalizing one, dissolving the hierarchy of classes by subordinating class conflict to a wider conception of social concern.

"Culture," by articulating right reason and developing the best self, creates within society an inner elect group which mediates the ideals of society. The standards of such a group ought to provide, Arnold feels, what the Academy in France ought to provide, without altogether succeeding, a criterion against which not simply literature, but social attitudes in general, may be measured. Such a culture liberalizes society by relaxing the anxieties of ignorant or bigoted concern. For it, moral and aesthetic standards are inseparable, united in the conception of good taste. Hence in the light of the cultured society, such behavior as the Catholic-baiting among nineteenth-century British Protestants can be seen to be, not simply wrong, but silly and vulgar as well. The impossibility of separating moral and aesthetic criteria indicates the importance of the critical function in society.

Arnold's argument gives a genuine social dimension to the study and teaching of the humanities, and does not, like Newman's, insist that we sell out to a concerned interest, such as the Christian Church. But when he comes to describe the *community* of culture, Arnold begins to sound less convincing, partly through his own honesty in recognizing that, while culture is at the centre of society, those who are at the centre with it are an isolated, in fact an alienated, group. With one hand Arnold writes of sweetness and light and of the one thing needful, which culture can provide; with the other he writes *Dover Beach* and *The Scholar Gypsy*, imaginative evidence that the happy few at the centre have become something more like a saving remnant.

Humanist education in the Renaissance was closely geared to social position: the students belonged mainly to the ascendant class, and were educated in the light of their future responsibilities, at least in theory. Victorian humanism, too, was inseparable from the conception of the "gentleman," who was emancipated from "working," in the class-conscious sense of that word. In nineteenth-century defences of Classical education, including Arnold's, the social context of education presents an issue that is often not squarely faced. To say that the

Classics are the source of much of Western culture, and of nearly all the more liberal part of it, is one kind of statement; to say that the study of the Classics should be a compulsory curriculum for everyone in quest of higher education is another. The Classical monopoly of education disappeared, but its social framework survived in the compulsory education which was growing up in Arnold's time, and which tended to standardize a course of study. The result was to carry over the two-tiered education, with an upper liberal level for gentlemen and a lower vocational one for others, into a society which was trying to outgrow such stereotypes.

In our day it has become accepted that everybody who has a genuine relation to society is a worker, consequently the term "gentleman" is no longer a socially functional term. The conception "gentleman's education," with which humanism was so long bound up, is no longer functional either. The tendency of democracy, ideally, is not so much to abolish an elite as to decentralize elites. In a society where everyone was at work, everybody would belong to an elite of some kind; and the survival of the older elitism in the notion that those who stay longest in school and go on to university get the "best" kind of education is obviously a considerable social nuisance. It is even more obvious that in the century since Arnold's book, the humanist society, which barely existed even then, has entirely disappeared. Arnold has had many successors who have followed him in his moral and judicial process of critical evaluation without noticing this fact. There are students of the humanities in universities and elsewhere, but that is not the same 'thing as a community of humanists. The mediating society which provides the norms for judging and evaluating literature has gone, and consequently each judicial critic can speak only for himself, though a merciful provision of nature may conceal from him the extent of his self-exposure. He may try to believe that his norms and values still exist in some kind of Platonic heaven, but even if they did they would not carry much authority. Today each intellectual is, socially speaking, in the position of Archimedes in Syracuse, who could perhaps move the world if he were standing in a different position, but, being where he is, is able to continue his work only so long as he is unnoticed by the murderous louts of Rome.

In tracing the development of the myths of concern and freedom, we come in humanism to a point at which they seem to interchange their original characteristics. The myth of concern takes on a reasoning aspect, claiming the support of logic and historical evidence; the myth of freedom becomes literary and imaginative, as the poet, excluded from primary authority in the myth of concern, finds his social function in a complementary activity, which liberalizes concern but also (apart from some tension here and there) reinforces it. The Romantic movement, as we shall see, brought in a quite different conception of the poet's role, but Marxism, in this century, has returned to the view of Sidney. Its programme for the arts is essentially protest before revolution, panegyric afterwards: once the revolution has been established, the artist's duty is to produce what we called in connection with Sidney a rhetorical analogue to Marxism, convincing the emotions and imagination of the validity of the socialist ideals which are more literally set out in Marxist philosophy and economics. Many of the best Russian writers do fall within this orbit, but the prescriptions of "social realism" have been notoriously incapable of coming to terms with much in modern art which is genuinely revolutionary in form, and not merely in content. The literary imagination is clearly the nucleus of the undeveloped myth of freedom in Soviet society.

Earlier in this discussion we quoted Ascham and Milton on the central belief of humanism in the social importance of disciplined speech. For Ascham, devoted to the principles of the Elizabethan settlement, good style, like law, was a manifestation of the order and security which church and state gave to society. Ascham may represent for us here all the conservative and usually classically-minded writers who need to feel, behind them, the reality of the spiritual and temporal authority which their writing manifests. Such writers find their social function in illuminating that authority for the social imagination. Dryden was, however, perhaps the last major writer who felt this reality in both spheres; after him, social authority becomes increasingly associated with an idealized conservatism or some intellectual construct like a "cultural tradition."

A good deal of literature after the Romantic movement reflects the conception of the writer's having assumed a spiritual authority by default, so to speak. Poetry, in particular, acquires the oracular, over-determined emotional resonance of something speaking authoritatively to an age that has most of its attention directed elsewhere. Romantic poetry, in Keats and Coleridge, preserves the sense of a charm or spell woven around some guarded place, and a corresponding sense of ritual separation from its audience. The later movement associated with Eliot, Pound, Hulme and Wyndham Lewis thought of itself as revolting against this attitude, but for the most part merely intensified it. Eliot followed a number of French predecessors in holding that if a tradition of authority had gone, it would have to be re-established before poetry could function properly, and in postulating "royalism" as a temporal counterpart to an established church. In others, including Mallarmé, Rilke, and perhaps Flaubert, there is rather a sense of the artist as a secular and initiating priest of a cultural tradition which preserves the lost authority of church and state in an ideal form. Wyndham Lewis, ridiculing what he called the "dithyrambic spectator," the member of the audience bumptious enough to imagine that his presence made any difference to the creative process, speaks from a similar position. In him and in many others, this reliance on an ideal order led to the exalting of archaic art, which the distance in time had tended to make inscrutably authoritative. The idealizing of the primitive suggests a certain affinity between modern art and modern religion: both become parts of a traditional myth of concern surviving as a kind of palladium or cultural monument, supported by a tolerance, even a respect, which is really based on indifference. The French Impressionists, excluded from the Academy, set up their own *"salon des refusés,"* but it is difficult even to imagine what sort of works of art would go into a *salon des refusés* today. Such tolerance, however, can hardly be supposed to mean that the authority of the arts has been generally accepted.

For Milton, on the other hand, so deeply suspicious of constituted authority in both church and state, the implications of the humanist attitude are very different. For him the relation of reality and appearance is reversed: it is constituted authority that is the outward manifestation of the real source of authority in society. The real source is the prophetic authority revealed in the inspired writer, which is derived from the Word of God. The impact of the Word of God on society, being a message from an infinite mind to a finite one, is always subversive and revolutionary. In Milton's view, the prophetic writer has recovered the poet's original role of teaching the myth of concern; and because of the revolutionary impact of the prophetic tradition, the message of concern is identical with the message of freedom. Liberty is what the will of God intends for man, but it is not anything that man naturally wants, his nature being perverted. What man naturally wants is either mastery or conformity to custom and to what we have been calling the anxiety of continuity. The prophetic writer is not just any good or even great writer, but the elect writer, whose devotion to his craft has extended to a dedication of himself as a prophet of God, and whose dedication has been accepted.

This conception of the prophetic poet as the medium of both the concern and the freedom of society is worked out in a Christian, and more particularly a Protestant, context by Milton, but its tradition is carried on outside that context by Shelley and others, and we shall have to examine it in the next section.

Four

As literature becomes assimilated to the mental habits of a writing culture, it comes to be thought of as an ornament of leisure, a secondary product of an advanced civilization. In the tenth book of Plato's *Republic*, Socrates asserts that the poet's version of reality is inferior, not merely to the philosopher's, but to the artisan's or craftsman's as well. The artisan makes what is, within the limits of his reality, a real bed; the painter has only the shadow of a bed. Most devaluations of poetry ever since, whether Platonic, Puritan, Marxist or Philistine, have been attached to some version of a work ethic which makes it a secondary or leisure-time activity; and when poetry has been socially accepted, it is normally accepted on the same assumptions, more positively regarded. This seems a curious conception of poetry in view of its original social role. In a technologically simple society preoccupied with the means of survival, like that of the Eskimos, poetry appears to be a primary need rather than a superfluous refinement. But increasingly, as Western culture became more complex, works of art came to be thought of as a series of objects to be enjoyed and appreciated by a liberalized leisure class.

A necessary part of this view of art is a decline of the sense of convention and, in poetry, of a community of words. The poet no longer has a communal "word-hoard," and only in the most subtle and indirect way is he thought of as possessing and retelling the essential myths of the society he lives in. The individual poem or novel comes rather to represent a unique or sealed-in experience, and a law of copyright assimilates literature to private property. Literature could not go as far in this direction as painting, where a picture acquires a purchaser or sole owner, but it went as far as it could. Kierkegaard, in contrasting Christian concern with the liberal and speculative attitude of his day, was so impressed by the similarity of the latter to the place of the arts in society that he called it the "aesthetic" attitude, and symbolized it by Mozart's *Don Giovanni*, more particularly by the catalogue of mistresses in that opera, the picture of the universal lover surrounded by a mass of attractive objects.

But as it became more "aesthetic," poetry began to be curtailed of some of its traditional attributes. Sidney's case for the poet depends on a body of generally accepted social ideas and values. As society becomes more confident about these values, the help of the poet in publicizing them becomes less essential. For Sidney, as we saw, the poet is potentially a religious teacher. In a later age, under Boileau's influence, the mysteries of religion are thought to be too high for the poet's ornamentation: on the other hand, the puerilities of heathen mythology are too low, and the poet should outgrow his hankering for them. Of the traditional qualities of oral poetry, the one that chiefly survives, in the age of Pope, is the sententious, the capacity to formulate "What oft was thought, but ne'er so well expressed." The high value set on this aspect of poetry continues well into Victorian times, partly because the sententious is a quality that assimilates poetry to prose. Otherwise, the elements that make Homer the cornerstone of our poetic tradition are precisely the elements that come to be most despised. Catalogues and lists and mnemonic verses of the "Thirty days hath September" type, quoted by Coleridge, are now regarded as poetry's lowest achievement: the formulaic unit becomes the cliché; the reverence for convention, of doing things because this is the way they are done, gives place to a reverence for "originality."

The poet's role of telling his society what his society should know also goes out of focus. The most intellectually tolerant of critics, studying the ideas or opinions of many major writers of the last century, is bound to be puzzled, even distressed, by the high proportion of freakish and obscurantist views he finds and the lack of contact they show with whatever the ideas are that actually do hold society together. In the twentieth century an important and significant writer may be reactionary or superstitious: the one thing apparently that he cannot be is a spokesman of ordinary social values. The popular poems of our day are usually poems of explicit statement, continuing the sententious tradition; but such poems seem as a rule to be out of touch with the real poetic idioms of their times. Recently, in an interviewing programme on the Canadian radio, a Toronto hippie remarked that the world would have no problems left if everyone would only read Kipling's "If" and live by it. One feels that in our day a remark of that kind could be attached only to a substandard poem.

Those who express the ideas and symbols that hold society together are no longer the poets; they are rather men of action with a power over the sententious utterance operating mainly outside literature, who usually arise in a revolutionary situation. Such men of action include Jefferson, and later Lincoln, in America, and the great Marxist leaders, Lenin and Mao. The "thoughts" of Mao in particular seem to have succeeded in putting Marxism into the aphoristic prose of concern, something that Marx himself rarely attempted after the Communist Manifesto.

The more completely the techniques of writing and the mental disciplines they create pervade a community, the more socially isolated poetry becomes. Prose grows into full maturity and in command of its characteristic powers, and thereby begins to break away from poetry, which has nothing like its capacity for conceptual expression. In proportion as scientific and philosophical pictures of the world develop, the starkly primitive nature of poetic thought stands out more clearly. One might have thought that, as the authority of science established itself, poets would become the heralds of science, as they had earlier been the heralds of religion. Many great poets, such as Dante, had in fact absorbed and used much of the science of their day. But after about Newton's time it became increasingly clear that most really important poets were not going to make much more than a random and occasional use of imagery derived from science or technology.

Many poets, naturally, have taken a keen and well informed interest in science, but it is true even of Shelley and Goethe that their best poetry does not really absorb scientific conceptions and vocabularies and express them with full poetic resonance. Cosmological and speculative themes have been central to poetry throughout its history, but versified science and abstract conceptual language have always been eccentric to it. There have been many efforts on the part of poets to get intellectually with it: there was the "aureate" pseudo-philosophical diction of fifteenth-century allegories, the Newtonian poetry of the early eighteenth century, and the "futurist" movement in the early twentieth. But all these trends, whatever their merits, also demonstrated that poetry has a limited capacity for abstract and technical language.

What had attracted earlier poets to the science contemporary with them was clearly not the science itself, but a certain schematic and mythical quality in it, associations of seven planets with seven metals and the like, which science itself eventually outgrew. This schematic quality, after about Newton's time, survived increasingly in a curious intellectual underground inhabited by occultists, theosophists, mystagogues, and the like. Yet this was where many poets turned for intellectual support. Further, as we see in Yeats, such interests are so triumphantly vindicated in the poetry itself that it seems clear that they are connected with the actual language of poetry, and are not simply a removable obstacle to appreciating it. Truth of correspondence grows and progresses, and each age of science stands on the shoulders of its predecessors; poetry knows nothing of progress, only of recurrence. Whatever science may say, the poet's world continues to be built out of a flat earth with a rising and setting sun, with four elements and an animate nature, the concrete world of emotions and sensations and fancies and transforming memories and dreams. Chemistry, with Boyle, becomes "skeptical" of the schematic constructs of alchemy, and eventually develops an elaborate periodical table of elements. But the four elements are still there in Dylan Thomas and the Eliot Quartets, and are likely to remain in poetry until that remote time in the future when chemistry, or whatever the appropriate science will then be, will have discovered that there are in fact four elements, and that their names are earth, air, fire, and water.

Apparently poetry cannot really escape the fact that it was

originally founded, not on the sense of an objective order of nature, but on the sense of social concern. Hence its approach to nature is primarily constructive and associational, and only becomes descriptive as a kind of *tour de force*. Poetry attempts to unite the physical environment to man through the most archaic of categories, the categories of analogy and identity, simile and metaphor, which the poet shares with the lunatic and the lover, and which are essentially the categories of magic. The figure of the magician, who, like Orpheus, can charm the trees by his song is a figure of the poet as well. The function of magic, said Pico della Mirandola, is to "marry the world" (*maritare mundum*), and this naive anthropomorphic image remains close to the centre of all poetic metaphor. But magic, as soon as writing develops, drops out of line with the rest of thought. Many other factors, too, such as ambiguity, which is a structural principle of poetry but simply means bad writing in any conceptual context, point to the fundamental incongruity between poetic and logical outlooks. No matter what compromises or social arrangements may be made, poetry speaks the language of myth and not the language of reason or fact: further, it represents something primitive in society, not something that progressively improves or refines itself.

In what sense is poetry "primitive?" Usually, the term is used historically, to mean something very early, or something that has survived unchanged from very early times. Certainly we have been talking so far about a historically primitive period, an oral culture in which the poet had a distinctive social role. And when the sense of the essential primitiveness of the poetic attitude revived in the eighteenth century, it is not surprising that it was accompanied, not only by the study of what were regarded as primitive literatures, such as Celtic and Norse, and not only by the revaluing of Homer as a primitive poet, but by actual pseudepigrapha like the Ossian and Rowley poems, contemporary writing ascribed to a remote past.

The other side of this primitivism is the anti-poetic myth of progress, which grew up around the same time, and after the publication of the *Origin of Species* took on some more sinister forms. The conception of evolution is of little use to a literary critic, for much the same reason that the measurement of a light year is of no use to a carpenter. Nothing justifies us in assuming that the contemporaries of the painters of Lascaux and Altamira were less intelligent than we are; our knowledge of literature does not go so far back; therefore criticism has to assume much the same standard of human ability for the entire history of literature. Unhappily, evolution came to be regarded as the scientific proof of a myth of progress, and the combination became, as has often been shown, part of an imperialist ideology, designed to rationalize the aggressiveness with which the white man assumed his burden.

According to the myth of progress, history shows a progress from primitive to civilized states, which turns out on investigation to be a progress in technology, though it is often called science. If two cultures collide, the one that gets enslaved or exterminated is the primitive one. The victorious one was more progressive because it had better weapons and armies— that is, it was better organized socially for destruction. It can often, of course, also prove that its people are more intelligent, because it is in a position to set the intelligence tests according to its own cultural pattern. The doctrine of progress embraced both a complacent comparison of Western societies to those in other parts of the world, and a parallel comparison of ourselves to our ancestors, as a means, as T. S. Eliot puts it, of disowning the past. Hence during the latter part of the nineteenth century, in particular, it came to be widely assumed that the rational or commonsense view of history was one that made all human beings as stupid as possible as recently as possible. It even reached the point of faking a "Piltdown man" to dramatize man's ascent from apelike savage to monkeying professor.

This conception of the "primitive" as meaning "inferior to us" is less fashionable now that it has become more obvious that the triumph of civilization, from its point of view, is also the possession of the means of total destruction. But it has been and still remains a considerable force. I often turn to a favorite book of my childhood, H. G. Wells's *Outline of History,* which is a fascinating source book for progressive mythology. There, the "outline of history" is appended to a brief introductory account of the evolution of life, on the assumption that history follows the same direction of development that evolution does. We read near the beginning of a Neanderthal man who was "quite a passable human being", in spite of not being able to walk erect "as all living men do". I understand that the evidence for this statement depended on a single specimen who was later proved to have had arthritis. The important thing for the present context is not the adequacy of the evidence, but the symmetry of a gradualist myth, in which somebody had to shamble before homo sapiens could walk upright. A gradualist myth of this form, in other words, needs inferior races, in order to lead up dramatically to the final epiphany of what Wells calls the "true men." Wells not being a fool, he does not identify these inferior races with Mongol hordes or the accursed progeny of Ham, so he puts them at the beginning of history, where they are both out of harm's way and are more convincingly related to their natural superiors, who have proved their superiority in two gradualist ways: by coming later and by still surviving.

One principle involved here is that nearly all popular historical myths are, like the myth of Christianity itself, related to comic romance, the story of the successfully achieved quest. As G. K. Chesterton remarks, the Victorians assimilated history to a three-volume novel, with themselves as the happily-ending third volume. Wells's post-Victorian version of this romance myth emphasizes the sequential structure inherent in all romance. The successful quest in romance is usually the third attempt, and in the passage referred to we have the evolution of man summarized in three stages. I dwell on this point here because the progressive perspective on culture, which sees it as a hierarchy of values with our own cultural norms on top and something that looks vaguely shaggy and brutish below, goes back to a form of snobbery which is really of humanist origin, and of which such historical terms as "Dark Ages" and "Enlightenment" are fossilized remnants.

The belief in the continuity and in the manifesting of an inner purpose in history, and in the movement of time generally, had been built into Western religious and political thought from the earliest times. It was still there in the culture of the nineteenth century, not only in its thought but in the long novels that rolled through complication and crisis to an inevitable conclusion, in the symphonies that took off from and returned to the same tonality, in the pictures that were moments of arrested movement, like the self-portraits of Van Gogh or the dancers of Dégas. The bourgeois progressive myth, which assumed a benevolent future on the whole, began to break down under the shocks of twentieth-century disasters, and the inherent paradox in the myth, that progress is a good thing and yet leads to increasing stability, became more obvious. Marxism could interpret the disasters more plausibly as the death-agonies of bourgeois culture, but while the two teleological myths continue to dominate much of our thinking, they do so increasingly out of habit rather than genuine conviction. The progress of science and technology produces an uneasy sense of a confused and rapid process of change that is just about to become clear: this sense has of course nothing to do with either science or technology, but is a social mirage, like flying saucers.

There is, however, a very cruel deception concealed in both bourgeois and Marxist progressive myths. Both project an ideal into the future; both can rationalize the most atrocious present acts as leading to a future good; both promise the gratitude of some hazy posterity for very real sacrifices of life and happiness to be made now; both present us with leaders who have the abstracted gaze of the car driver, looking away from the immediate community into the imminent; both constantly tell us that we can really enjoy the blessings of our civilization only after some particular social hurdle is got over first. The "we can't do this until" formula seems plausible until we start noticing that there is a series of hurdles, that the series never comes to an end, and that an earlier religious view was probably more realistic in assuming that the temporary hurdle could only be life itself, and could only be cleared by death. In the society of our day the unhappiest people are those who, in Sir Charles Snow's phrase, have the future in their bones: who convince themselves, every night, that Godot will infallibly come tomorrow.

The myth of gradualism comes increasingly to be a reflection of what suggested it in the first place: the fact that science advances and progresses, and that the technology which science makes possible affects human life in a progressive way. Whether this latter form of progress is always an improvement or not depends on what aspects of it are selected for argument. Few of us want to go back to medieval dentistry or plumbing, but as soon as the standard of improvement declines from the humanist "refinement of manners" to technological convenience, some ambivalence arises. Most gradualist myths assume a greater freedom in the future through the shifting of drudgery from men to machines; experience notices an increase of legislative restriction in response to every major technological change, such as the invention of the automobile, a steady pressing of life into the mechanistic patterns suggested by the machines themselves. Hence among the poets, in particular, a strong movement takes shape, of the type that Snow, in the essay glanced at above, calls "Luddite". The Luddite tendency is really a protest against the mechanical dehumanizing of life, however, and it only looks reactionary when its opposite is assumed to be beneficent.

This brings us to the kind of primitivism which is more directly characteristic of poetry, where the term "primitive" is used rather in a psychological sense. Man driving a car, writing at a desk, playing golf or selling razor blades is civilized or technological man. Man admiring a sunset, quarrelling with his wife, demonstrating for peace or committing suicide is primitive man. That is, he is man preoccupied with the existential situation of his own humanity, with the emotions, speculations, hopes, despairs, and desires which belong to that situation. Even in Sidney, in his appreciation of the ballad of Chevy Chase or his famous phrase about the poet coming to us "with a tale which holdeth children from play, and old men from the chimney corner," we are reminded that there is always something primitive about poetry in this sense. Poetry is continually bringing us back to the starting-point, not necessarily of time, but of social attitude. And as society becomes more dominated by mechanical and technological features, and as a myth of progress tends increasingly to alienate the poet from his society, the poet's conception of his social role changes accordingly.

Humanism thought of the writer, at least the established

writer, as socially an insider, near the centre of his society. The typical humanist strives to be sane, balanced, judicious; he is not a prophet nor an angry man, nor does he seek a transvaluation of values. He avoids both technical and colloquial language, and has a deep respect for conventions, both social and literary. As a professional rhetorician, his instinct is to save the face of the situations he encounters by finding the appropriate words for them. Grace and tact, for him, are not mere accomplishments: they are evidence of the social importance of a literary training. If we compare such an attitude with that of, say, Ezra Pound, we can see how far a creative and imaginative writer of our time has moved from the traditional humanist position. Pound is a Classical scholar with most of the humanist attitudes and interests, including the view that disciplined verbal utterance is essential to the welfare of society, a view he associates with Confucius. What is different is his place in society, by which I mean something more fundamental than the fact that he is an expatriate who has been accused of treason. The latter was also true of Dante, who was much closer to traditional humanism. It is rather that Pound's admiration for Mussolini was a somewhat pathetic effort to adopt a viable social role, and the failure of the effort was not merely personal but was symbolic of a profound malaise in contemporary society. Other poets have tried to attach themselves to left-wing causes, often with equally futile or tragic results. The significant writer today is not necessarily an exile, expatriate, or martyr, though a disconcerting number of modern writers have had these roles, but he seldom seems to be geared to the social machinery, wherever he is.

D. H. Lawrence is another writer whose opposition to the mechanizing of life has taken a psychologically primitive form. Much of Lawrence's work, like much of Wordsworth's, really belongs to the pastoral convention, and stresses a fundamental kinship between human and physical nature which a good many aspects of civilized life have betrayed or denied. As we can see in *The Plumed Serpent* and elsewhere, the psychologically primitive tends to lapse into the historically primitive, to a quixotic return to idealized earlier types of society, when visualized as a goal of social action. The regressive myth in Lawrence has much the relation to his pastoral vision that the "noble savage" myth has to Rousseau's conception of a natural society. That is, it is separable from his real social vision—"in details I'm sure I'm wrong," as he says in one of his letters. In his strange essays on the unconscious, again, we see how the force which the poet opposes to the enslaving of man by his own technology is the mythopoeic imagination, the associative and constructive creative power as it operates in words. Everywhere in Lawrence, as with most major writers of our time, we see that the poet cannot become the focus of a myth of freedom. Poets have always been the children of concern: they still show a liking for being converted to dogmatic creeds of all kinds, sometimes with the greatest contempt for the toleration they receive; they are a competitive and traditionally an irritable group; their genius is one of intensity rather than wisdom or serenity.

The tradition associating the poet with an existential protest against the increased mechanizing of life goes back in English literature to Blake, with his "dark Satanic mills" and his vision of society as a machine

> . . . wheel without wheel, with cogs tyrannic
> Moving by compulsion each other.

Blake links this growth of tyranny with Lockian philosophy and Newtonian science. For an attitude which begins in the detached study of nature or an objective world is very apt to end in a conviction that moral law is, or ought to be, as predictable as natural law. One can trace similar attitudes in Milton, what with the technological interests he gives to Satan, and his very ambiguous treatment of Galileo in *Paradise Lost*. Shelley, in the notes to *Queen Mab*, was later to say that the "miserable tale" which is the subject of Milton's epic is inconsistent with knowledge of the stars, and it is not impossible that some feeling that Galileo represents an element in the human mind that might eventually blow up the whole story of Adam and Eve was close to Milton's own consciousness. At any rate, Adam is certainly not encouraged to devote too much attention to the stars. Thus again the mythopoeic imagination is the force opposed by Milton and Blake to what they both, in different ways, consider Satanic. And just as Matthew Arnold is the last of the great humanists, so the turning point toward the present anti-technological attitude of the artist is marked by Ruskin, who also shows a profound interest in the cultural importance of mythology.

For some time science has been regarded as something that might, if transmuted into "scientism", or a similar form of progressive mythology, provide the basis for a new and very sinister myth of concern. A century ago Samuel Butler expressed a preference for Christianity over any such new scientism, without having much belief in either, on the ground that it would be a disaster to exchange an old and sophisticated myth, which had been deprived of its inquisitorial powers and been forced to come to terms with tolerance and suspended judgment, for a young and naively dogmatic one, which preferred the temporary excitement of change to considering the consequences of the change. The nightmare of a conspiracy which has retained one element of science, the element of predictability, and used it as a means of imposing a permanent tyranny in society is one of the commonest themes of recent fiction, especially science fiction, where sometimes (e.g. in Ray Bradbury's *Fahrenheit 451*) the cause of freedom is represented by the artist. This completes the interchange of functions that begins with humanism, where the elements of the myth of freedom are seen as perverted into a conspiracy to betray freedom, which only the artist is left to defend.

The new recognition of the primitive and mythical nature of poetry is the essential point that Peacock seizes on in his brilliant satire *The Four Ages of Poetry*, perhaps the nearest to Vico of any piece of writing in English literature. Here Peacock pretends to accept the assumption that mankind progresses through reason to greater enlightenment, and shows on the basis of this assumption that poetry, like the less interesting types of religion, is committed to the values of an outworn past. In other words, he identifies the primitive element in poetry with the historically primitive, and builds his paradoxes on that. According to Peacock, poetry began in early times as "the mental rattle that awakened the attention of intellect in the infancy of civil society." The chief form of primitive poetry was, Peacock says, panegyric, which points to the identification of the poet with his community that we find in oral cultures. Poetry has its greatest flowering, or golden age, in the times immediately following, when habits of thought are still close to the primitive. But as civilization develops, Plato's prophecy becomes fulfilled, and the poet becomes more and more of an atavistic survival. "A poet in our times is a semi-barbarian in a civilized community. He lives in the days that are past. His ideas, thoughts, feelings, associations, are all with barbarous manners, obsolete customs, and exploded superstitions. The march of his intellect is like that of a crab, backward."

With the rise of the Romantic movement, and its interest in the ballad and other forms of primitive verbal culture, its use of superstition and magic as poetic imagery, its withdrawal from urban culture and its tendency to seek its subjects in the simplest kinds of rural life, the historical cycle has run its course. The poet can hardly be a teacher of a society he does not even understand. "As to that small portion of our contemporary poetry . . . which, for want of a better name, may be called ethical, the most distinguished portion of it, consisting merely of querulous, egotistical rhapsodies, to express the writer's high dissatisfaction with the world and every thing in it, serves only to confirm what has been said of the semi-barbarous character of poets, who from singing dithyrambics and 'Io Triumphe', while society was savage, grow rabid, and out of their element, as it becomes polished and enlightened." Peacock's reference is to the Romantic poets, but the statement is hardly less true, within its ironic context, a century later.

Shelley's defence, though it looks as though it were ignoring Peacock's thesis, actually provides a close and searching answer to it. The main point of the answer consists in the shifting of the emphasis from the historically to the psychologically primitive. Shelley begins by neatly inverting the hierarchy of values assumed in Sidney. Sidney is concerned to show that poetry is a genuine instrument of education, along with religion, morality and law, but their claim to be educational is prior and unquestioned. Shelley puts all the discursive disciplines into an inferior group of "analytic" operations of reason. They are aggressive; they think of ideas as weapons; they seek the irrefutable argument, which keeps eluding them because all arguments are theses, and theses are half-truths implying their own opposites. Some of the discursive writers are defenders of the social status quo: not only do they fail to defend it, but they exasperate and embitter a society in which the rich get richer and the poor poorer. There are also liberal and radical discursive writers: they are on Shelley's side and he approves of them, but being only the other half of the argumentative disciplines, the amount of good they can do is limited. The works of imagination, by contrast, cannot be refuted: poetry is the dialectic of love, which treats everything it encounters as another form of itself, and never attacks, only includes. Thus there appears in Shelley, as in his predecessors, the conception of a model world above the existing world. This model world for him, however, is associated not with the Christian unfallen world, nor even with the Classical Golden Age, in spite of some allusions to the latter in the *Defence,* but rather with the higher reason, *Vernunft* as distinct from *Verstand,* which so many Romantics identified with the imagination.

This argument assumes, not only that the language of poetry is mythical, but that poetry, in its totality, is in fact society's real myth of concern, and that the poet is still the teacher of that myth. He may be an "unacknowledged legislator," but he is still the lawgiver of civilization, as in ancient times, even if nobody realizes it. There is a reality out there, a reality which is given and has in itself no moral significance, which the lower understanding studies, and there is the reality which does not exist to begin with, but is brought into being through a certain kind of creative activity. The metaphor of creation, if it is a metaphor, is not new with the Romantics, and most of the better Elizabethan critics understood what is meant by "creative" very well. But in Sidney's day it was accepted that the models of creation were established by God: for Shelley, man makes his own civilization, and at the centre of man's creation are the poets, whose work provides the models of human society. The myths of poetry embody and express man's creation of his own culture, rather than his reception of it from a divine source.

The imagination thus reverses the direction of the tragedy of Mary Shelley's *Frankenstein,* the story of how man enslaves himself to what he creates. A religion, considered as a creed and as a social institution, is, for Shelley, a projected, and consequently a perverted, creation of the human imagination. The creative element in literature is therefore connected essentially with the recovery by the imagination of what it has projected. There is no question of a poem's being a rhetorical analogue to historical or moral or religious truth, and the expression of poetry is no longer thought of as improved or developed by rhetorical training, which undercuts a central humanist conception. The poet's authority is derived from the oracular power in his mind that was formerly ascribed to God's revelation. This power is "that imperial faculty, whose th·one is curtained within the invisible nature of man." It is clear from such a phrase that a new conception of rhetoric is forming, one which is based on intensity of emotional feeling rather than on craftsmanship and calculated effects, like the rhetoric of Spenser, or for that matter of Milton.

Poetry, says Shelley, is "that to which all science must be referred." The mythical *confronts* the logical, assimilating it to the concerns of human existence. The act of imaginative recovery of what was formerly projected into religion thus separates the created reality of poetry from the presented reality of the objective world. Poetry "defeats the curse which binds us to be subjected to the accident of surrounding impressions." One implication here, which takes us beyond Shelley, is that there are two cultures in society, one the main area of the sciences, the other an area covered by something that we are here calling mythology. They co-exist, but are not essentially interconnected.

The more immediate implication is that the poetic and the revolutionary impulses are interdependent. The primitive nature of poetry does not make it reactionary: it makes it rather, as we saw, the human protest against the dehumanizing elements in society. Our perception of a given reality, the world out there, tends to become habitual, hence a pernicious mental habit develops of regarding the unchanging as the unchangeable, and of assimilating human life to a conception of predictable order. But poetry, Shelley says, "creates anew the universe, after it has been annihilated in our minds by the recurrence of impressions blunted by reiteration." The imagination, which conceives the forms of human society, is the source of the power to change that society.

Every great poem is a product of its time, and is consequently subject to the anxieties of its time. It is essential to Shelley's argument that the authentic reading of poetry reads it by its imaginative "underthought" and not by its explicit conformity to contemporary prejudice, or what he calls, in connection with Calderon, "the rigidly-defined and ever-repeated idealisms of a distorted superstition." If, for instance, we read Dante's *Inferno* as a poem designed to increase our anxieties about a life of unending torment after death awaiting most of those who do not make an acceptable deal with the Church, then, from Shelley's normal point of view, writing such a poem would be an act of treachery to the human race far lower than anything done by Dante's three traitors, Brutus, Cassius, and Judas Iscariot, all of whom must have acted from better motives. But, of course, we read the *Inferno* through its imagery and action, as a representation of the actual life of man, and as such it instantly becomes overwhelmingly relevant, not a malicious and superstitious nightmare. We quoted a critic earlier as calling *Paradise Lost* a monument to dead ideas. There are no dead ideas in literature; there are only tired readers. When the imagination is doing the reading, it operates in a counter-historical direction—it redeems time, to use a phrase which is Shelleyan as well as Biblical, if in a different context—and literature for it exists totally in the present tense as a total form of verbal imagination. Shelley speaks of this total form as "that great poem, which all poets, like the co-operating thoughts of one great mind, have built up since the beginning of the world." The lightning flash of this image illuminates the contemporary critic's *pons asinorum,* the bridge leading over to the other shore of criticism, where the social context and reference of criticism is to be found.

We saw that the conception of the critic as the judge or evaluator of literature makes sense only in relation to a humanist elite society which operates within an established framework of concern. When this society disappears, the critic has to abandon this function, and see what his real function is. The argument of this section has led us to the view that literature represents the *language* of human concern. Literature is not itself a myth of concern, but it displays the imaginative possibilities of concern, the total range of verbal fictions and models and images and metaphors out of which all myths of concern are constructed. The modern critic is therefore a student of mythology, and his total subject embraces not merely literature, but the areas of concern which the mythical language of construction and belief enters and informs. These areas constitute the mythological subjects, and they include large parts of religion, philosophy, political theory, and the social sciences.

Students of mythology often acquire the primitive qualities of mythopoeic poets. I have read a good many of them, from medieval writers through Bacon and Henry Reynolds and Warburton and Jacob Bryant and Ruskin to our own time, and I have noted two things in particular. First, a high proportion of them are cranks, even nuts, and, second, they often show a superstitious reverence for the "wisdom of the ancients." These qualities are not hard to account for: their crankiness is partly the result of the intensely associative quality of myth, where almost any kind of analogy may be significant, and their respect for antiquity is connected with the fact that literature does not improve, but revolves around its classics. Even the greatest mythological explorers of the last generation, Frazer and Freud, are apt to sound dated as soon as they attempt to be rational. The modern critic's approach, however, is, in the terms of my opening section, not allegorical but archetypal: he seeks not so much to explain a poem in terms of its external relation to history or philosophy, but to preserve its identity as a poem and see it in its total mythological context. Hence the critic *qua* critic is not himself concerned but detached. His criteria are those of the myth of freedom, depending on evidence and verification wherever they come into the picture. (The implication, that concern can be studied with detachment, we shall have to examine in the next section.) Once the critic is released from the preoccupations of a moral and evaluating approach, he is obliged to preserve a tolerance for every variety of poetic expression and a respect for every poet's individuality. Such a phrase as "of course I don't like this *kind* of poetry" can never be uttered by a serious critic.

According to Shelley the poets of the past have been subject to the anxieties of their times, but there is also a way of reading poetry that redeems it from these anxieties and sees it in its context as a part of the total poem that the human imagination has made. The critic, however, is in the opposite cultural situation from the poet: he is subject to the anxieties of *his* time, and it is the poet's relation to the poet's own age that is the liberal element in the critic's study. The critic dealing with Shakespeare, let us say, has to try to grasp the implications of the fact that Shakespeare still holds the stage and still communicates with the present age, for reasons that would have been unintelligible to most of Shakespeare's contemporaries and quite probably to Shakespeare himself. At the same time Shakespeare lived in a specific age and addressed a specific audience which was remote from ours in cultural assumptions. The attempt to understand Shakespeare somewhat as his contemporaries may be supposed to have understood him brings us into contact with an alien culture and expands our own notions of cultural possibilities. (I am not assuming the elementary fallacy that all reactions in 1600 would be alike, only that all of them, like all of ours, revolved in the same cultural orbit.) Shakespeare's relation to us is that of one more voice of concern, speaking with the authority of what Wallace Stevens calls the essential poem at the centre of things. It is not a contemporary voice, and it has the oracular quality of something definitively revealed in the past. The critic has to establish a pattern of continuity linking present culture with its heritage, and therefore with its inheritors, for a culture that is careless of its past has no defences against the future. As a historical critic he continues the humanist tradition, which owed so much of its liberal quality to the fact that it studied a vanished culture with detachment, uncommitted to its religious and political concern. As a contemporary he is a student of our own concern, and has to see how the past bears on it.

The crux of the critic's problem is in his attitude to what we have been calling the model world, and which we should now call the imaginative world. It is obvious that for Shelley, as for Milton before him, concern and freedom are the same thing, and the poet's message proclaims both at once. But to the extent that the poet is a liberator, Shelley's imaginative world becomes a potentially existent world, something to be brought into being by a certain kind of social action. As

Shelley has no very clear notion of what such action should be, his message of freedom comes to us, not with the trumpet of a prophecy, but with the shrill, hectoring voice of anxiety, and in the didactic tone which he elsewhere calls, more shrewdly if less truthfully, his abhorrence. What is true of Shelley's poetry is true *mutatis mutandis* of all poetry: it can express concerned protest, but for the elements of a myth of freedom we must look elsewhere. Literature is the embodiment of a language, not of belief or thought: it will say anything, and therefore in a sense it says nothing. It provides the technical resources for formulating the myths of concern, but does not itself formulate: for formulation we must turn from literature back to the myths of concern themselves.

The humanist ideal offered a "liberal" education to those who were economically liberated: for it, the study of the greatest achievements of humanity provided the only genuine vision of freedom that society possessed. As the social focus of education slowly shifted from a community of gentlemen released from servile work to a community in which everyone is some kind of worker, the artist took on a new social importance as the model for the worker. Genuine work, which dignifies the worker by uniting him to his society, is distinguished from labor or drudgery, which humiliates because there is always a large element of exploitation in it. This distinction is developed out of Carlyle by Ruskin, in whom work is identified with creative act, with what expresses the identity of the worker. Parallel arguments could be drawn from the early work of Marx, including the Communist Manifesto, though I find it hard to accept the neo-humanistic Marx that is sometimes reconstructed from them, but Ruskin is closer to the present issue. In William Morris the conception of work as creative act combines with some revolutionary features of an anarchist cast. For Morris, the "major" arts, including literature, have some social associations of ruling-class privilege about them; the "minor" or practical arts are potentially revolutionary, because they relate art directly to social conditions, and their development can help to break down the drudgery and exploitation of factory and machine production and transform society into a community of brains and hands.

Morris perhaps never escaped from a social paradox in his own life: his practice as a designer, much as it diversified the Victorian cultural scene, did not really illustrate his theories. The voice was the voice of a revolutionary Esau, but the hands were the hands of a smooth and accommodating Jacob. In spite of this, Morris in *News from Nowhere* gives a picture of a "liberal" education which is the radical counterpart to Arnold's humanism, and is in many respects almost disconcertingly contemporary. Education in Morris's dream world is practical, active, entirely voluntary, and un-bookish. It is even anti-intellectual: scholars are tolerated, but they are an oddity. A greater contrast to Arnold's reading and thinking humanist contemplating the best that has been thought and said would be difficult to imagine than this super-kindergarten where everyone is digging and building and picnicking and whittling. The only humanist feature is the *sprezzatura* that does work as though it were play (which it is on the Tom Sawyer principle, as nobody is obliged to work).

The reason for such an emphasis in this book is dramatically appropriate: Morris's people are not simply children let out of school; they have been let out of history, the prison of the past with its treadmills of war and slavery. The one form of the anxiety of continuity that deeply affected Morris, the preservation of old buildings, is resolved when man stops allowing machines to enslave him and so recovers the power of good design. Thus, just as Arnold sums up the "Classical" humanist conception of culture, so Morris comes nearest to summing up the "Romantic" conception of culture as the primitive revulsion against the mechanizing of life. Toward the end of the book, however, the heroine remarks that it is probably a mistake to neglect history and scholarship as much as they do, because "happy as we are, times may alter; we may be bitten with some impulse towards change, and many things may seem too wonderful for us to resist, too exciting not to catch at, if we do not know that they are but phases of what has been before."

The primary safeguard of freedom, then, is even in Morris the contemplative element in education which is science in its primary sense of *scientia*, the study of the world presented to the mind. The rest of Morris's book, on the other hand, demonstrates that part, and an essential part, of the sense of freedom comes from the release of the creative imagination. It is still true that literature is the embodiment of a language rather than of belief or thought. But there is a point at which the analogy with language breaks down. Nobody would accept a conception of literature as a mere dictionary or grammar of symbols and images which tells us nothing in itself. Everyone deeply devoted to literature knows that it says something, and says something as a whole, not only in its individual works. In turning from formulated belief to imagination we get glimpses of a concern behind concern, of intuitions of human nature and destiny that have inspired the great religious and revolutionary movements of history. Precisely because its variety is infinite, literature suggests an encyclopaedic range of concern greater than any formulation of concern in religious or political myth can express. The examining of this expanding of the mind as we move from concern to imagination is the fifth stage of our critical path.

Five

___

We may perhaps arrive at some tentative conclusions from our quasi-historical survey before we turn to the contemporary scene. In the first place, the great dream of the deductive synthesis, in which faith and knowledge are indissolubly linked, seems to be fading. The confidence in the completeness and adequacy of the Thomist synthesis, expressed so eloquently by Maritain in the last generation, is clearly not what it was in this more fragmented age. In Marxism it is obvious that the deductive synthesis, whenever it has become socially established, comes to depend more and more for its support on third-rate bureaucrats rather than on first-rate writers or thinkers. Evidently we must come to terms with the fact that mythical and logical languages are distinct. The vision of things as they could or should be certainly has to depend on the vision of things as they are. But what is between them is not so much a point of contact as an existential gap, a revolutionary and transforming act of choice. The beliefs we hold and the kind of society we try to construct are chosen from infinite possibilities, and the notion that our choices are inevitably connected with things as they are, whether through the mind of God or the constitution of nature, always turns out to be an illusion of habit. The mythical and the factual or logical attitudes are really connected by analogy. If, for example, such a philosopher as Bergson or Lloyd Morgan bases a metaphysical or religious structure on the conception of evolution, what he is working with is not really the same principle as the biological hypothesis of evolution, but is rather a mythical analogy of that hypothesis.

It seems equally futile to expect any one myth of concern to establish itself all over the world. The more widely any such myth spreads, the deeper the rifts that develop within it. One reason for this is that concern, if unchecked by any internal or intellectual opposition, must have an enemy. Marxist countries must have imperialistic aggressors; bourgeois societies must have Communist subversives, just as medieval Christendom had to have a pretext for starting the Crusades. We said earlier that a myth of concern draws a *temenos* or spellbinding line around a society. This bounding line has two aspects. A society enriches itself by what it includes; it defines itself by what it excludes. Whether or not good fences make good neighbours, the fence creates the neighbour. In *A Passage to India* E. M. Forster shows us how three great cultural complexes, Hinduism, Islam and Christianity, each accept ideals of universal brotherhood; their better and more sensitive members believe in these ideals and struggle to achieve them. And yet in the long run they all define themselves by exclusion, and those who do not wish to exclude anything run the risk of losing their identity and having their total inclusiveness turn into its terrible opposite, the sense of a totally meaningless universe, the ironic vision of the absurd, which comes to Mrs. Moore in the cave.

The only practicable solution seems to be the one hit on by democracy when it was trying to pare the claws of Christian temporal power. This is to accept, as part of a permanent tension between concern and freedom, a plurality of myths of concern, in which the state assumes the responsibility for keeping the peace among them. I return here to a distinction I have made elsewhere between closed and open mythologies. A society with a closed myth of concern makes it compulsory for all its citizens to say that they support it, or at least will not overtly oppose it. Only a society with an open mythology is capable of a genuine and functional toleration. There are limits to toleration, of course, but the distinction between a society that imposes a belief and a society that imposes a kind of rules-of-the-game order within which dissent and opposition can operate is a practical distinction, however difficult to formulate in theory.

We saw earlier that every myth of concern is religious, in the sense of establishing a *religio* or common body of acts and beliefs for the community. Such a religion may be theistic and deny the finality of death, like Christianity, or atheistic and assert it, like Marxism. Marxism, and Christianity as long as it had temporal power, have tended to assume that a definite position on such points was obligatory on society as a whole, and hence, even if they could tolerate a group with a different position, they could not recognize such a difference as inevitable, certainly not as desirable. The tendency of a closed myth is to move from such broad general principles to more specific ones, prescribing more and more of a citizen's beliefs, and obliterating the varieties of social attitude. Jews, for instance, are a minority group with a myth of concern peculiar to themselves: consequently any society with a closed myth which contains Jews is bound sooner or later to turn anti-Semitic. Occasionally we find it suggested that breaking up closed myths of concern may be part of the historical function of Judaism. The King of Persia complains, in (the Greek additions to) The Book of Esther: "in all nations throughout the world there is scattered a certain malicious people, that have laws contrary to all nations . . . so as the uniting of our kingdoms, honorably intended by us, cannot go forward."

A society with an open mythology may still have its own predominant myth of concern. Nobody would say that "the American way of life" was less concerned than any other community's way of life. The principle of openness, however, is, so far as I can see, the only possible basis for a world community, assuming that no myth of concern can ever become world-wide. What is potentially world-wide is an assumption, too broad in itself to constitute a myth of concern, that life is better than death, freedom better than slavery, happiness better than misery, health better than sickness, for all men everywhere without exception. A society with an open myth can accommodate itself to such an assumption; a society with a closed one cannot. The latter can only pursue its own ends, deciding at each step how much misery and slavery may be necessary (of course only temporarily, it is always added) to advance those ends.

An open mythology establishes the relativity of each myth of concern within it, and so emphasizes the element of construct or imaginative vision in the myth. This would not affect the reality of, say, the Christian myth for anyone who holds it, but it puts it on the kind of basis on which communication, or what is now often called "dialogue," becomes possible with Jews or Moslems or Marxists, or even other Christians. When a myth of concern claims truth of correspondence as well as truth of vision, and assumes that its postulates are or can be established as facts, it can hardly produce any "dialogue" except the single exasperated formula: "But can't you *see* how wrong you are?" When it renounces this claim, it acquires the kind of humility which makes it possible to see intellectual honesty on the other side too. As for one's own side, one is not renouncing its truth: what one renounces is the finality of one's own understanding of that truth.

In all societies the pressure in the direction of a closed myth is also the tendency within society to become a mob, that is, a social body without individuals or critical attitudes, united by slogans or clichés against some focus of hatred. A myth of concern, by itself, cannot prevent this kind of social degeneration. Faith, or participation in a myth of concern, is not in itself verifiable, but to some extent it can be verified in experience. Some myths of concern obviously make a fuller life possible than others do. Charity, in the sense of respect for human life, is doubtless the primary criterion, but there is an important secondary one: the ability of a myth of concern to come to terms with the myth of freedom. A faith which permits intellectual honesty is clearly better in practice than one which tries to deny elementary facts of history or science. And perhaps the two standards, of charity and of intellectual honesty, are ultimately the same standard. Certainly such a myth of concern as Nazism, which ranks so low on the scale of charity, could not avoid the falsifying of history and science, and I suspect that the two vices always go together.

The basis of all tolerance in society, the condition in which a plurality of concerns can co-exist, is the recognition of the tension between concern and freedom. This issue becomes crucial as soon as it is obvious that the study of man's environment cannot be confined to the non-human environment. Human society, in the present as in the past, is an objective fact too. Sooner or later, therefore, the scientific spirit and the search for truth of correspondence will invade the structures of concern themselves, studying human mythology in the same spirit that they study nature. This collision between concern and freedom may well be the most important kind of what is now called "culture shock" that we have. In weak or insecure minds such a collision produces immediate panic, followed by elaborate defensive reactions. Efforts to bring the spirit of inquiry into the Christian religion meet with such responses as (to give a relatively mild example): "If you destroy our faith with your rational and analytical questions, what will you put in its place?" Many Marxist theologians similarly insist that, as everybody exists in a specific social context, there is no such thing as complete detachment from a social attitude, and consequently all inquiry is rooted in a social attitude which must be either revolutionary, and so in agreement with them, or counter-revolutionary. One still often hears the argument among student militants and others that because complete objectivity is impossible, differences in degree of objectivity are not significant.

It would be a grave error to associate this kind of resistance only with the immature or the easily frightened. We all have such fears, and can look at them in perspective only from a later historical age, when battles previously fought have since been won, or at least stopped. Meanwhile, it is clearly one of the unavoidable responsibilities of educated people to show by example that beliefs may be held and examined at the same time. We noted the encyclopaedic drive of concern: there is nothing that is not the concern of concern, and similarly there is nothing that can be excluded from free inquiry and the truth of correspondence. Concern and freedom both occupy the whole of the same universe: they interpenetrate, and it is no good trying to set up boundary stones. Some, of course, meet the collision of concern and freedom from the opposite side, with a naive rationalism which expects that before long all myths of concern will be outgrown and only the appeal to reason and evidence and experiment will be taken seriously. I hope it is clear from the general argument of this essay why I consider such a view entirely impossible. The growth of non-mythical knowledge tends to eliminate the incredible from belief, and helps to shape the myth of concern according to the outlines of what experience finds possible and vision desirable. But the growth of knowledge cannot in itself provide us with the social vision which will suggest what we should do with our knowledge.

This is where the central question of the present essay, the social function of criticism, comes in. Let us follow up this problem of the examining of a myth of concern by the standards of a myth of freedom, and see what happens as a result. The obvious example to choose is Christianity and the myth centered in the Bible. Within the last century there has been a crisis in the response to the Biblical Christian myth which is often called a crisis of belief, but is really a crisis in understanding the language of belief. The crisis begins in Victorian times, and immediately provokes the kind of resistance that one expects at the beginning of such a movement. In Newman's lectures on education, particularly in connection with science, we see how calmly reasonable the tone is as long as mathematics and the physical sciences are being discussed, and how edgy and nervous it becomes as soon liberal theology begins to appear, however distantly, on the horizon. Then we are sharply warned that science ought not to go beyond its province and invade the field of religion. Matthew Arnold, though holding an entirely different view of religion, reacted quite as strongly to the iconoclastic attacks of Bishop Colenso on the historicity of the Pentateuch. It was wrong to confuse science and religion; it was wrong to take such matters to the general public, because only a few are capable, etc.; above all it was wrong to write crudely and bluntly about these subjects, as Colenso did. However, of course, the movement proceeded in spite of such resistance.

When I am asked if I "believe in" ghosts, I usually reply that ghosts, from all accounts, appear to be matters of experience rather than of belief, and that so far I have had no experience of them. But the fact that the question takes such a form indicates that belief is usually connected in the mind with a vision of possibilities, of what might or could be true. On the other hand, we often use the term "believe" to mean a suspended sense experience. "I believe you will find a telephone on the next floor" means that if I were on the next floor I should see a telephone. In reference to past time this suspended sense experience becomes the acceptance of a historical fact. "I believe Julius Caesar existed" implies that I think that if I had lived when and where he is said to have lived I should have seen him. "I believe in God" can hardly refer to a belief of this kind, but under the influence of the mental habits of a writing culture, concerned belief also has come to be associated with historical fact.

This leads to such curious aberrations as "believing the Bible," i.e., of ascribing special virtue to asserting that in another culture, a few years ago and a few miles away, Jonah was swallowed by a great fish and Elijah carried up to heaven in a fiery chariot, and that if we had been present at those events we should have seen precisely what is described in the sacred text. Such belief is really a voluntarily induced schizophrenia, and is probably a fruitful source of the infantilism and the hysterical anxieties about belief which are so frequently found in the neighborhood of religion, at least in its more uncritical areas. One thinks of Don Quixote's remark to Sancho Panza, that the Golden Age would soon return if people would only see things as they are, and not allow themselves to be deluded by enchanters who make hundred-armed giants look like windmills.

In the seventeenth century Sir Thomas Browne, reflecting on such matters as the fact that conditions in Noah's ark, after thirty-eight days or so, might become a trifle slummy, remarked "methinks there be not enough impossibilities in religion for an active faith." But of course when a faith beyond reason is looked at in this sort of playful or ironic light, it tends to become unconcerned. The more genuinely concerned faith is, the more quickly a hierarchy is established in it, in which "essential" beliefs are retained and less essential ones regarded as expendable. But this conception of "essential" belief is, in spite of the word, introducing an existential element into belief. What we really believe is not what we say or think we believe but what our actions show that we believe, and no belief which is not an axiom of behavior is a genuinely concerned belief. Marxism has a similar conception of unessential belief, the "ideology" which is to be talked about but not acted upon, and which has the function of decorating the facade of a conservative attitude. Many of my readers would call what I am calling a myth of concern an ideology, and though, as I have indicated, I have specific reasons for using the term myth, those who prefer ideology may substitute it in most contexts.

For Milton writing *Paradise Lost* Adam and Eve were historical characters, his own literal ancestors, and Milton is fond of contrasting the plain and sober Scriptural accounts with the extravagances of the heathen. Simplicity however is not an infallible sign of historical credibility, and we today are struck rather by the similarity of the Biblical stories of the fall and the flood to other myths in other cultures. As the Old Testament narrative proceeds, myth gives place to legend and what German critics call *Sage*, legend to historical reminiscence, historical reminiscence to didactic and manipulated history, and so on. But there are no clear boundary lines: all that seems clear is that whatever in the Old Testament may be historically accurate is not there because it is historically accurate, but for quite different reasons. Further, historical accuracy has no relation to spiritual significance. The Book of Job, which is avowedly an imaginative drama, is clearly more significant in the development of religion than the begats in Chronicles, which may well contain authentic records.

With the Gospels, however, surely things must be different, for Christianity has always insisted on the historical nature of its central event. We soon begin to wonder, however, whether the verbal presentation of that event is as historical as the event itself. We notice that the life of Christ in the Gospels ·is not presented biographically, as a piece of continuous prose writing founded on historical evidence, but as a discontinuous sequence of appearances (pericopes), which have a strongly mythical quality about them. If the approach were biographical we should want only one definitive Gospel, and of course the historical belief in them has always rested on some "harmony" of their narratives rather than on the four as they stand.

Naturally many efforts have been made to extract a credible continuous narrative from what seems a mass of mythical accretions. Thus a century ago Ernest Renan, in his *Vie de Jésus,* began confidently with the statement that Jesus was born in Nazareth, the story that he was born in Bethlehem having been inserted later to harmonize with Micah's prophecy that the Messiah was to be born in Bethlehem. But, arguing on those terms, if the only reason for associating Jesus with Bethlehem is the passage in Micah, the only reason for associating him with Galilee is a similar passage in Isaiah (ix), and the only reason for associating him with Nazareth is to enable Matthew to make a dubious pun on "Nazirite." Renan's historical and credible statement, on his own basis of argument, dissolves into two more myths.

As we go through the Gospels, with their miracles of healing and miraculous feeding and raising the dead and the like, we begin to wonder how much there is that must be historical, that is unambiguous evidence for a historical Jesus. The authors of the Gospels seem to care nothing for the kind of evidence that would interest a biographer; the only evidence they concern themselves with is coincidence with Old Testament prophecies of the Messiah. The result is that our historical evidence for the life of Jesus, besides being hermetically sealed within the New Testament, seems to melt away, as we try to grasp it, into echoes from the Old Testament or from contemporary Jewish ritual. As some factual basis for Jesus's life was obviously available to the authors, why did they make so oblique and limited a use of it?

For any uncommitted reader of the Gospels, the question "could it really have happened just like that?" is bound to occur with great frequency. But at a certain point the question begins to turn into the form: "if I had been there, is that what I should have seen and experienced?" At this point the doubts become overwhelming, because most of these doubts are of one's own capacity for spiritual experience. Sir Thomas Browne's "I thank God that I never saw Christ or his disciples" begins to sound like a very shrewd remark. If I had been out on the hills of Bethlehem on the night of the birth of Christ, with the angels singing to the shepherds, I think that I should not have heard any angels singing. The reason why I think so is that I do not hear them now, and there is no reason to suppose that they have stopped.

If, under the influence of the mental habits of a writing culture, we insist on regarding a myth as a disguised way of presenting a real situation, we should have to regard the accounts of Jesus in the Gospels as highly suspect, if not actually fraudulent. But the impression of authority they convey is too strong to take the possibility of fraud seriously. It is much more probable that it is our conception of myth that is wrong, and it seems better to think of the authors as too concerned about the importance of their message to entrust what they had to say to merely historical or biographical idioms of language. The historian tries to put his reader where the event is, in the past. If he is writing about the assassination of Julius Caesar, he tries to make us see what we should have seen if we had been there, while keeping the additional understanding afforded by the distance in time. The apostle feels that if we had been "there," we should have seen nothing, or seen something utterly commonplace, or missed the whole significance of what we did see. So he comes to us, with his ritual drama of a Messiah, presenting a speaking picture which has to be, as Paul says, spiritually discerned.

Myth is the language of the present tense, even of what is expressed by the vogue-word "confrontation." There is a moral aspect of literature, stressed by Sidney among others, which literature possesses through its power of idealized example. When poetry is the "companion of camps," a heroic achievement in the past is linked to another in the future of which the reader is the potential hero. The best way to connect the two, for Sidney, is to present the former in its universal shape, combining the historical example with the abstract precept or model. If we wish to be inspired by Achilles we must read Homer, and may well thank God that we never saw Achilles or his myrmidons. Of course the historical criticism of the

Bible plays the same liberalizing role here that it does else-where: it helps to ensure that a book set in an ancient Near Eastern culture, remote from ours in language and social assumptions, can never be completely kidnapped by provincial bigotry in our day. But the direct connection of religion with concern, where "go thou and do likewise" is always a part of the presentation, decreases the importance of this.

The Bible, it may be said, is not a story-book or an epic poem; but it is much closer to being a work of literature than it is to being a work of history or doctrine, and the kind of mental response that we bring to poetry has to be in the forefront of our understanding of it. This is, I think, what Matthew Arnold meant when he suggested that poetry would increasingly take on a religious importance in modern culture. It is not that poetry will become a substitute or replacement for religion, a situation that could only produce phony literature as well as a phony religion. It is rather that religion will come to be under-stood increasingly as having a poetic rather than a rational language, and that it can be more effectively taught and learned through the imagination than through doctrine or history. Imagination is not in itself concern, but for a culture with a highly developed sense of fact and of the limits of experience, the road to concern runs through the language of imagination.

What applies to the Bible applies also, in some degree, to every scripture of concern, from the Vedic hymns to the Communist Manifesto. One question that arises is evidently the relation of myth to the ordinary standards of truth of corre-spondence. The connection between the growth of a myth of concern and the falsifying of history is so frequent as to be the rule, and it is not merely a vulgarizing of language that has given the word "mythical" the overtones of "false." When we see a myth of concern in process of formation, as with the con-temporary black myth, we can see that rigid adherence to historical or sociological fact may not be the only moral principle involved.

There is also the conflict of loyalties between the demands of objective truth and the demands of concerned tactics, especially, in our day, the tactics of publicity. I remember a friend who was deeply committed to what he felt was a genuine social issue, and found himself watching a carefully rigged scene in which a member of his side produced an impression, for the benefit of television cameras, of being brutally beaten by members of the other side. He was told that this kind of thing was tactically necessary, with the implication that if he so much as remembered that he saw what he did see he was working for the other side. A properly disciplined faith, perhaps, would forget, rationalize, or make no account of the total unreality of the incident. One would surely have a much higher opinion, however, of a person who felt, as my friend felt, some sense of violated integrity. It seems curious that hardly anybody rejects the values of contemporary civilization to the point of disbelieving in the necessity or effectiveness of public relations. Yet the invariable tendency of public relations, whatever they are working for, is to destroy the critical intelligence and its sense of the gap between appearance and reality. Bertrand Russell remarked in an interview just before his death that the skeptical element in him was stronger than the positive one, but "when you're in propaganda you have to make positive statements." He was clearly implying that the skeptical side of him would have considered many of his positive statements false if he had allowed it to do so. A more disturbing question is whether there can ever be truth of concern that is not in some degree falsehood of correspondence; whether myth must lie, and whether there can be any piety, to whatever church or state, without some kind of pious fraud.

Certainly in a world as complicated as ours there is bound

to be the kind of oversimplifying tactic that may be called concerned tokenism. One of the commonest features of concern is the anxiety, usually conservative, that finds a symbolic focus in some change of fashion or custom. A history of preaching would include a long record of thunderous denunciations of new fashions in clothes or entertainment, where there has clearly been an unconscious choice of something relatively trivial to represent the devil's master plan to destroy mankind. Even yet, the few square inches of the body still covered on bathing beaches can serve as an intense focus of anxiety for the anxious. But even serious concern has to pick one issue out of many, and sometimes the disproportion between the concern and the chosen issue indicates the ascendancy of rhetoric over reality that is an element in all lying. Thus Bryan's "you shall not crucify mankind upon a cross of gold" sounds a trifle over-apocalyptic for the fact that his party had decided to fight an election on the issue of bimetallism. And while one may not warmly sympathize with Arnold's attitude to the deceased wife's sister bill in *Culture and Anarchy*, one does have to recognize the existence of deceased-wife's-sister liberalism (or radicalism or conservatism): the choosing of an issue more or less at random, not only to satisfy the need for action but to serve as a symbolic anxiety-substitute for a more demanding concern. All scapegoat figures, from Shelley's king and priest to Ezra Pound's usurers, are symbolic substitutes of this kind.

We have recurrently found throughout this discussion that there is an element in concern that resists final or ultimate formulation. Every myth of concern, as we pursue it, eventually retreats from what can be believed to what can be imagined. It seems clear that the standards of a myth of freedom, the standards of logic and evidence and a sense of objective reality, are also approximations. They too are analogies of a model world that may not exist, yet they must be there as ideals of procedure, however impossible it may be to realize them completely. In times of stress the inadequacy or impossibility of objective truth, and the consequent necessity of noble lies, is much insisted on, though as a rule with a kind of bravado that indicates some self-hypnotism. The original noble lie, in Plato's *Republic,* was to the effect that some men are golden, others silver, others of base metal. I suspect that every tactically necessary lie is a variant of the Platonic one, and has for its ultimate end the setting up of a hierarchy in which some people are assumed to be of more human worth than others. As Orwell's *1984* in particular has so trenchantly shown, lying weakens the will power, and therefore the will to resist being taken over by a police state.

There is also a philosophical issue involved which concerns the degree to which anything in words can tell the truth at all, in terms of the truth as correspondence. In truth of correspondence a verbal structure is aligned with the phenomena it describes, but every verbal structure contains mythical and fictional features simply because it is a verbal structure. Even the subject-predicate-object relationship is a verbal fiction, and arises from the conditions of grammar, not from those of the subject being studied. Then again, anything presented in words has a narrative shape (*mythos*) and is partly conditioned by the demands of narrative. These demands are those of a verbal causality which is *sui generis,* and has no direct connexion with any other kind of causality or sequence of events. To go further with this subject would take another book, and one that I am not in the least competent to write, although it would deal with a central issue of literary criticism. Some less ambitious considerations may be dealt with here.

We have seen that the integrity of the Bible as a myth has

a good deal to do with its unreliability as history. Its relation to doctrine and concept is very similar. The conceptual aspect of the Bible is presented mainly in the discontinuous or concerned prose that we have already discussed, in such forms as commandment, oracle, proverb, parable, pericope, dialogue, and fable. Once again we see that the Biblical tradition adheres closely to its oral origin. A body of teachings presented in this way, assuming an overall coherence, can readily be systematized, that is, translated into the sequential and continuous prose of doctrine. But, like the "underthought" of poetry, it resists the *definitive* synthesis, because the discontinuity indicates other contexts than that of logical or sequential connexion. So the question arises, to what other contexts do such statements of concern belong?

In theistic religions, God speaks and man listens. Neither conception is simple, for all the efforts to make them so. God speaks, by hypothesis, in *accommodated* language, putting his thoughts and commandments into a humanly comprehensible form. Once the primary revelation is received, in prophecy or gospel or sura or oracle, man's listening takes the form of interpretation, which means critical reconstruction. There is no "literal" way of receiving a message from an infinite mind in finite language. So every myth of concern, even if it is assumed to start with the voice of God himself, is involved by its own nature in a complex operation of critical commentary.

Statements of belief or concern are existential, and therefore one very obvious context for them, apart from doctrinal synthesis, is the life of the person who makes or inspires them, and who is usually a leader or culture-hero of some kind. In religious leaders particularly we notice the link with the oral tradition. Jesus, Buddha, even Mohammed, do not write, but make their utterances usually in connexion with specific occasions, some of their disciples acting as secretaries, like the author of the collection of sayings of Jesus (Q) which is pre-served in Matthew and Luke. Once a myth of concern is socially established, the personal focus falls on the leader or interpreter who is centrally responsible for sustaining the myth in history.

This line of succession may derive from such figures as Paul, whose letters, like the pamphlets of Lenin later, deal with specific tactical decisions in a way that leads to far-reaching theoretical principles. Or it may take the form of a succession of leaders who are regarded as definitive interpreters of the myth of concern, like the Pope with his *ex cathedra* infallibility in Catholic Christianity or the Marxist leaders. Such leaders are regarded as incarnations of a dialectic, like Plato's philoso-pher-king. In other contexts the incarnation may be a purely symbolic figure like Elizabeth II, in her role of "defender of the faith." The most primitive form of such a conception is the kind represented by the *Führerprinzip* of Nazism. A much more open and sophisticated one is that of the Constitution of the United States, which was theoretically dictated by an inspired people to a prophetic group of founding fathers. When two myths of concern collide, this personal focus is usually prominent in the collision. It was the repudiation of the largely symbolic cult of the deified Caesar that marked Christians and Jews off from the Roman world; and when Julian the Apostate tried to set up a more philosophical and "open" alternative to Christianity he could hardly avoid putting his own cult at the centre of it.

The earlier stages of a myth of concern usually include a development of an oracular and mainly oral philosophy, as-sociated with wise men, prophets or gurus whose sayings may also be recorded, often very haphazardly, by disciples or scribes. A strong esoteric tendency to distinguish between an inner and an outer court of hearers, or between deep and shallow comprehension of the same doctrines, is notable here. The practice of reserving special teachings for a smaller group of initiates has run through philosophy from Pythagoras to ·Wittgenstein. Similar esoteric movements make their way, sometimes in the form of philosophical heresies, into the great religions, producing various Gnostic developments in Christianity, Sufism in Islam, and what eventually became the Mahayana form of Buddhism. A secret tradition, believed to be authentically derived from the same source as the exoteric one, but possessing qualities that the latter would fear and distrust, may serve as a kind of back door or fire escape for a myth of freedom in persecuting times.

Any personality at the centre of a myth of concern whose life is the context of a body of teaching must be regarded as having reached a definitive level of truth. But as truth of concern is not truth of correspondence, and cannot be verified and expanded like the established principles of a science, it follows that such a central personality is bound to create a hierarchy of response. This hierarchy of response is often represented, as above, by an inner group of specially enlightened followers. But in a socially ascendant myth it tends to become formalized in an institution, which becomes the acknowledged interpreter of the myth of concern, again on a hierarchical basis.

The more open the myth, the more the task of interpreting it begins to show analogies to literary criticism. The myth of concern usually exists as a body of words drawn up in the past, sometimes a remote past, and this body of words is, like the critic's text, unalterable. The variable factor is the new social situation provided by the interpreter's age; and, as there is an indefinite series of such new situations, it follows that the original structure, again like the critic's text, is not only unalterable but must be inexhaustible in reference. Thus the Supreme Court in America may not alter the Constitution, but must say what an eighteenth-century principle means in a twentieth-century world. The assumption is that the principles are comprehensive enough to be applicable to any current situation.

We notice that in this interpreting process what may have been originally sequential or systematic arguments tend to break down into a discontinuous series of general principles, each of which acquires a different context in the commentary attached to it. In other words it acquires the detached oracular structure of the prose of concern. Such commentary is of course very similar to criticism in literature, and it is clear that the different forms of critical interpretation cannot be sharply separated, whether they are applied to the plays of Shakespeare, the manuscripts of the Bible, the American Constitution, or the oral traditions of an aboriginal tribe. In the area of general concern they converge, however widely the technical contexts in law, theology, literature or anthropology may differ.

The analogy of literary criticism to the interpreting of a myth of concern suggests that statements of belief or concern can have a literary context as well as the existential one of a leader's life. In literature such statements have the context of a story, from which they emerge as comments or applications. From a literary point of view every statement of belief or concern can be seen as the moral of a fable. We referred earlier to the importance of the sententious element in literature: for centuries epigrams on the human situation, embedded in a Classical author, were regarded as the pearls of literature, worth opening the oyster to get. We also noted a social and intellectual contrast in the forms of concerned prose between oracular statements, the dark sayings of the wise, which tend to be esoteric in reference, and proverbs, which tend to be the expression of popular wisdom and to circulate in gregarious swarms, there being something about the proverb, in all ages, that seems to stir the collector's instinct. It is not surprising that in later literature we find oracular aphorisms more frequently attached to tragedies and proverbial ones to comedy and satire. The fable traditionally has a moral at the end: the convention of *beginning* a story with a sententious comment, already well established in Boccaccio, appears in *Rasselas* and is expanded into a major feature of *Tom Jones*. It is still going strong in the opening sentences of *Anna Karenina* and (in the key of delicate parody) *Pride and Prejudice*.

On a larger scale, statements of Christian belief are inseparable from the story of the Bible, which in its literary aspect is a comic romance. Similarly the Greek belief in fate, or whatever was meant by such words as ananke, moira, and heimarmene, is essentially chorus comment on the narrative form of tragedy which the Greeks invented. In our day we tend to go from the three R's in our education to a belief in, or at least an assent to, the three A's: anxiety, alienation, and absurdity. But these concepts again are noble sentiments derived from a prevailingly ironic age of fable.

When Raphael in *Paradise Lost* was sent down to talk to Adam, the reason for sending him was to impress Adam with the importance of not touching the forbidden tree. Raphael, however, refers only obliquely to the tree: what he mainly does is to tell Adam the story of the fall of Satan. The implication is that teaching through parable, the typical method of Jesus, is the appropriate way of educating a free man, like Adam before his fall. After his fall, Adam gets from Michael a similar emblematic and illustrative instruction, though within his new and fallen category of linear time, where the events are prophecies of an inevitable future to him, records of an inescapable past to the reader. Yet education is still by story or "speaking picture," with morals attached, and the total containing structure of the teaching is the Christian romantic comedy of salvation. Angels, evidently, teach by fable; teaching by morals is merely human, and only the officially and institutionally human at that.

Educating through the fable rather than through the moral involves all the responsibilities of a greater freedom, including the responsibility of rejecting censorship. Of all the things that Milton says about censorship in the *Areopagitica,* the most far-reaching in its implications seems to me to be his remark that a wise man will make a better use of an idle pamphlet than a fool would of Holy Scripture. That is, the reader himself is responsible for the moral quality of what he reads, and it is the desire to dodge this responsibility, either on one's own behalf or that of others, that produces censorship. Statements of concern are either right or wrong, which means, as the truth involved is not directly verifiable, that they are accepted as right or wrong. For the deeply concerned, all arguments are personal, in a bad sense, because all arguments are either for them or against them, and hence their proponent, to be acclaimed or refuted, needs simply to be identified as one of us or one of the enemy. In a tense situation within an open myth of concern, when pressure groups are starting up to try to close it, the formula "you only say that because you're a (whatever is appropriate)" is often regarded as penetrating the reality behind a hypocritical facade. The preservation of the open myth depends on giving the foreground of impersonal argument its own validity; the other direction leads inevitably to censorship and an *index expurgatorius.* One sees the hierarchical institution beginning to take shape here, with the censors forming an elite.

The most unattractive quality of the censor is his contempt for other people. The censor says: "I want this play banned, because, while it can't possibly do me any harm, there are all those people over there who will be irreparably damaged in their morals if they see it." Similarly, the person who attaches a smear label to whatever he disagrees with is really saying: "It may be all very well to appeal to me with logical arguments, because I can see through them; but there are all those people over there who are not so astute." The same habit of mind is common among those who are anxious to save themselves trouble in thinking or reading. I note in several Freudian books a tendency to describe Freudian revisionists or heretics as "reactionary." I mention Freud because he was in so many respects a conservative, pessimistic, even "reactionary" thinker who has been made into the founder of a myth of revolutionary optimism. The implication is that calling anyone a reactionary, or any similar epithet, if it relates to qualities assumed to be inherent in his work, is intellectually dishonest. Nobody's *work* is inherently revolutionary or reactionary, whatever the writer's own views in his lifetime: it is the use made of the work which determines what it is, and any writer may be potentially useful to anybody, in any way.

A more difficult assumption of responsibility relates to the writer's beliefs, and the particular concerns that he participates in. We have already met the principle that in reading poetry the "overthought," or explicit statement, is expendable to some degree, and that the "underthought" or progression of image and metaphor is the decisive meaning. When a myth of concern is derived from the teachings of a single man, or series of accredited teachers, those teachers must be regarded as in a very special sense wise or inspired men. No such respect need be accorded the poet so far as he represents a belief or attitude, however important and essential the belief may be to the poet himself. Hopkins and Claudel would probably never have bothered to keep on writing poetry without the drive of a powerful Catholic belief; but what makes them poets is their skill in using the language of concern, and hence they can be studied with the greatest devotion by readers who share none of their commitments. Still, most reasonable readers would respect a Catholic belief, whatever their own: a much more crucial example would be, say, Céline, who is a significant and important writer to many readers who could not possibly regard his views with anything but contempt.

The principles involved here are, first, that while the teacher of a myth of concern must be a wise or great or inspired man to his followers, the poet, or speaker of the language of concern, may be an important poet, and yet, in certain other respects, almost any kind of a damned fool. Second, the subordination of reader to poet is tactical only: he studies his author with full attention, but the end at which he aims is a transfer of the poet's vision to himself. Poetry is not, then, to be merely enjoyed and appreciated, but to be possessed as well. Third, there are no negative visions: all poets are potentially positive contributors to man's body of vision, and no *index expurgatorius* or literary hell (to use Milton's figure in *Areopagitica*) exists on any basis acceptable to a student of literature. Therefore, fourth, criticism does not aim at evaluation, which always means that the critic wants to get into the concern game himself, choosing a canon out of literature and so making literature a single gigantic allegory of his own anxieties.

We spoke earlier, however, of a canonical group of myths at the centre of an oral verbal culture. As writing, secular literature, and a myth of concern develop, the language of concern shifts to the conceptual, the statement of belief. Doctrine and creed replace such formulas as "in the eternal dream time." Meanwhile, literature goes its own way, continuing to produce stories, images and metaphors. When the critic arrives at the stage indicated by Shelley's *Defence*, of being able to conceive of literature as a totality, an imaginative body and not simply

an aggregate, the centrifugal movements of concern and literature begin to come together again. The critic begins to see
literature as presenting the range of imaginative possibilities of
belief, its stories the encyclopaedia of visions of human life and
destiny which form the context of belief.

"The Old and New Testaments are the Great Code of Art,"
said Blake, indicating the context of his own work, and similarly literature is the "great code" of concern. Many mythical
stories, like those of the fall or the flood, seem increasingly
puerile when one tries to rationalize or historicize them, but
approached in the universalized terms of the imagination, they
become conceivable as visionary sources of belief. Other myths
of concern, democratic, Marxist, or what not, are also founded
on visions of human life with a generic literary shape, usually
comic. Literature as a whole is also, like religious and political
movements, to be related to a central life, but its central life is
the life of humanity, and its inspired teacher the verbal imagination of man. Once again, literature in its totality is not a
super-myth of concern, truer because more comprehensive than
all existing ones combined. Literature is not to be believed in:
there is no "religion of poetry": the whole point about literature
is that it has no direct connection with belief. That is why it
has such a vast importance in indicating the horizons beyond
all formulations of belief, in pointing to an infinite total concern
that can never be expressed, but only indicated in the variety
of the arts themselves.

In modern times the classical statement of the relation of
concern and freedom is Kierkegaard's *Either/Or,* from which
the existentialist traditions of our day mainly descend. For
Kierkegaard the detached, liberal, and impersonal attitude
fostered by the study of an objective environment, and which
flowers into comprehensive intellectual systems like that of
Hegel, is an "aesthetic" attitude. It is fundamentally immature

because with this attitude man tries to fit himself into a larger container, the general outlines of which he can see with his reason, but forgetting that his reason built the container. The crisis of life comes when we pass over into the commitment represented by "or," take up our primary concern, and thus enter the sphere of genuine personality and ethical freedom.

The postulates of Kierkegaard's ethical freedom are Christian postulates, and his commitment is an acceptance of faith. The acceptance is fundamentally uncritical, because, so the argument runs, man is not a spectator of his own life. But, we saw, the context of Christian faith is a context of vision and fable and myth, and Kierkegaard does not really come to terms with the implications of this fact. Milton's portrayal of Adam looking at the sequence of Adamic life presented in the Bible, where the Christian faith becomes a total informing vision which Adam contemplates as a spectator, shows a far profounder grasp, not only of Christianity, but of the whole problem of concern. If we stop with the voluntary self-blinkering of commitment, we are no better off than the "aesthetic": on the other side of "or" is another step to be taken, a step from the committed to the creative, from iconoclastic concern to what the literary critic above all ought to be able to see, that in literature man *is* a spectator of his own life, or at least of the larger vision in which his life is contained. This vision is nothing external to himself and is not born out of nature or any objective environment. Yet it is not subjective either, because it is produced by the power of imaginative communication, the power that enables men, in Aristotle's phrase, not merely to come together to form a social life, but to remain together to form the good life.

What applies to a Christian commitment in Kierkegaard applies also to commitments to other myths of concern, where Kierkegaard's "aesthetic" would be replaced by "escapist" or "idealistic" or what not. Kierkegaard is saying, in our terms, that concern is primary and freedom a derivation from it, as the present discussion has also maintained. The individual who does not understand the primacy of concern, the fact that we belong to something before we are anything, is, it is quite true, in a falsely individualized position, and his "aesthetic" attitude may well be parasitic. But Kierkegaard, like so many deeply concerned people, is also saying that passing over to concern gives us the genuine form of freedom, that concern and freedom are ultimately the same thing. This is the bait attached to all "either-or" arguments, but it does not make the hook any more digestible.

It is worth pausing a moment on this point, because Kierkegaard is not really satisfied with his own argument. He clearly understood the fact that freedom can only be realized in the individual, and sought for a Christianity that would escape from what he calls "Christendom," the merely social conformity or *religio* of Christianity. He speaks of the personal as in itself a subversive and revolutionary force, and sees the threat of what we should now call the totalitarian mob in the "impersonal." For him the highest form of truth is personally possessed truth, and he is not afraid to face the implications of what I think of as the "paranoia principle." This is the principle, lurking in all conceptions of a personal truth transcending the truth of concern, that it is only what is true only for me that is really true. This principle brings us back to the conception of a definitive experience, which we met at the end of the first section, as an unattained reality of which literature appears to be an analogy.

Concern raises the question of belief, and belief raises the question of authority, the question "Who says so?" I have tried to show that the authority of concern, in itself, is always the authority of a social establishment. Even if its answer is "God says so," its effective answer is always "it doesn't matter who originally said so: we say so now, and you will accept it or else." It is different with the authority of reason and evidence and repeatable experiment: granted that there is no absolute objectivity, etc., it is still true that this kind of authority is the only genuine form of spiritual authority. That is, it is the only kind of authority that enhances, instead of encroaching on, the dignity and the freedom of the individual who accepts it. Unless the autonomy of this kind of authority is fully recognized and respected, there can be no escape from "Christendom" or whatever other conforming mob may be thrown up by concern. What I have been calling an open mythology is really the recognition of this autonomy, a readiness on the part of society to accept a "both-and" rather than an "either-or" situation.

The context of the myth of freedom is the environment of physical nature, and this environment is one of alienation, a sub-moral and sub-human world. Concern is an essential part of the attempt to escape from this alienation by forming a human community. The myth of freedom is born from concern, and can never replace concern or exist without it; nevertheless it creates a tension against it. One necessary development of this tension is the collision between the two kinds of authority when a myth of concern is approached from the standards of a myth of freedom. What emerges from the conflict is the sense of an imaginative world as forming the wider context of belief, a total potential of myth from which every specific myth of concern has been crystallized. The imaginative world opens up for us a new dimension of freedom, in which the individual finds himself again, detached but not separated from his community. Hence, though we cannot simply accept the view of

Shelley that the poetic imagination speaks the language of freedom as well as concern, still one essential aspect of freedom
is the release of the language of concern, or allowing freedom
to the poetic imagination.

Again, this new dimension of freedom, which includes the
released imagination, cannot take the place of concern: we can
neither live continuously in the imaginative world nor bring it
into existence. The tension has to continue. But maintaining
the tension is difficult, like standing on a pinnacle, and there
are constant temptations to throw ourselves off. The temptation
listened to by Kierkegaard, and by so many existentialists and
others since, is the temptation to identify freedom with the
power of choice. As we can really choose only what commits
us, this means that, like Adam in Eden, we can express our
freedom only by annihilating it. This is an irony of the human
situation. But irony, as students of literature realize, is not the
centre of human reality but only one of several modes of imaginative expression, and it is a function of the critic to provide
some perspective for irony.

Irony in literature has a great deal to do with a conception
of freedom which identifies freedom with freedom of the will.
Such freedom is usually thought of as opposed to necessity,
and the irony consists in the fact that such freedom eventually
collapses into the fatality it tries to fight against. If we associate
a free will of this kind with God, we embark on that dismal
theological chess game that ends with predestination in time,
with the God of Burns's Holy Willie who

> Sends ane to heaven and ten to hell
> A' for thy glory

and whom anyone less obsessed with concern would find great
difficulty in distinguishing from the devil. If we associate it
with an individual, he soon becomes a tyrant who acts by

whim and caprice, and so is not free but a slave of his own compulsions. If we associate it with a society, we get the kind of "will of the people" which is mob rule, where the leaders play the same enslaving role that compulsions do in the tyrant. The only genuine freedom is a freedom of the will which is informed by a vision, and this vision can only come to us through the intellect and the imagination, and through the arts and sciences which embody them, the analogies of whatever truth and beauty we can reach. In this kind of freedom the opposition to necessity disappears: for scientists and artists and scholars, as such, what they want to do and what they have to do become the same thing. This is the core of the freedom that no concern can ever include or replace, and everything else that we associate with freedom proceeds from it.

Six

We get two kinds of education in life. The primary kind is an education in concern, an understanding of the axioms and assumptions on which the people around us act, or say they act. It is an education in loyalties, attachments, beliefs, responses, and ideals, though later it may be modified by a growing sense of dissonance between professed and genuine beliefs, between ideals and realities. We study relatively little of it, and get most of it out of the air from our parents, teachers, and contemporaries. But every society has ways of ensuring that we learn it, and learn it thoroughly and early, even though some aspects of it, such as the teaching of religion, may be left to private enterprise. The fact that in America today one is free to be of whatever religion one pleases, or of no religion at all, means that religion, in its specialized sense, is no longer a central area of social concern. The situation is very different with what is called the American way of life, where there is a powerful pressure toward conformity.

This education in concern is followed by, or goes along with, a secondary education, mainly in the truth of correspondence, which is education properly speaking, and is the chief business of schools and universities. From the universities in particular, the concern of the educated minority, which is centered on the myth of freedom, leaks out to society as a whole. In a society that has what I have called an open mythology, there is a certain critical element in education, which consists in becoming increasingly aware of one's own mythological conditioning. Some of the subjects studied in the university are the mythological subjects, and they include the myths of concern belonging to the society in which they are studied.

Whatever the theoretical complications, the distinction between studying a myth of concern and promoting it is quite familiar in practice. A publicly supported university is assumed to teach a religion within the orbit of the truth of correspondence, presenting it simply as a faith that as a matter of historical fact has been or is held. Similarly, the university's role with other myths of concern is to study, for example, Marxism, but not to support the kind of "seminar" on Marxism which consists only of charging the batteries of the Marxist faithful, and which is really a kind of religious service. The same principle applies to the myth of democracy itself: it is not the function of a university to indoctrinate even that myth, because the public indoctrination of any myth tends to close it.

Something of the difference in social atmosphere between open and closed mythologies is perhaps expressed by the difference between the words advertising and propaganda. Advertising implies a competitive market and an absence of monopoly; propaganda implies a centralizing of power. If advertising is selling soap we know that it is only *a* soap, not the exclusive way of cleanliness. Hence the statements of advertising contain a residual irony. They are not expected to be literally believed by normal adults, and the gullible and impressionable audience which advertising assumes is a largely fictitious one. Such advertising is generally recognized to be a kind of game: it is hypocrisy in the original sense of acting a part. In religion and politics there is, one hopes, less hypocrisy, but some residual irony is still there in the competition of parties and "denominations." Irony is however an adult and individual attitude, a considerable strain to keep up, and for weaker members the narcotic charm of self-hypnotism, which is essential in totalitarian societies, has a strong attraction. Thus in Thomas Pynchon's brilliant satire, *The Crying of Lot 49*, an announcer, finding that he cannot pronounce such formulas as "rich, chocolaty goodness" with the requisite sincerity, goes on drugs, which disintegrate him as an individual and turn him into a voice of the mob.

The principle of openness in a myth of concern does not, we said, prevent a society from having a central myth of concern. What it does do is to break up what is so often called its "monolithic" aspect. Expressions of faith in the closed myth of medieval Christianity ranged from the philosophy of St. Thomas Aquinas to the crudest forms of relic fetishism. But all intense orthodoxy, however subtle or sophisticated on its highest levels, rests on a compromise with less enlightened versions of the same views. The latter can be deprecated, but not repudiated. Erasmus may ridicule or Luther denounce the popularity of indulgences and relics, but the Council of Trent must reaffirm the genuineness of these phenomena. Our own society is less orthodox in that sense. As in all societies, we are first introduced in childhood to popular social mythology, the steady rain of clichés and prejudices and assumptions that come to us from elementary schooling, from mass media, from entertainment, from conversation and gossip. In a society with an open mythology this process has little if any conscious aim, but unconsciously it aims, very precisely, at the same goal as that consciously sought in societies with closed myths, that is, the docile and obedient (or "adjusted") citizen. A few years ago (things have improved lately) the bulk of American education up to about grade eight was essentially an education in the clichés of American social mythology, the teaching of what purported to be literature being almost entirely so. But in an open mythology we encounter, as we go up the educational ladder, other forms of social mythology, some confirming the more elementary ones, others rejecting or repudiating them.

The situation has the great advantage, not merely of keeping American social mythology open, but of making a critical attitude toward that mythology, along with the education which fosters the attitude, functional in society. It has the disadvantage of making disillusionment so much a part of social education that it may leave one's permanent loyalties unformulated and undefined. There are those who accept American social mythology uncritically; there are those who reject much of it in theory but come to terms with it in practice, and there are those who repudiate it in practice but are unable to say where their real loyalties belong. Much of the social energy that a myth of concern generates leaks away through the openings of critical and analytical attitudes. This is not a bad thing in itself, as a free society must have these attitudes, but it creates other problems.

For example, American society is usually called a "capitalist" society, especially in Communist countries. The belief in capitalism, so far as capitalism commands a belief, appears to rest mainly on an analogy between laissez-faire and liberalism, between the entrepreneur and the creative, adventurous or emancipated individual, of the kind that the phrase "free enterprise" suggests. This analogy is deeply embedded in the elementary social mythology I just referred to, and of course many Americans hold it for life. Others find it dishonest, or, at best, vague and unconvincing, and feel that social education involves outgrowing it. In general, it is perhaps true to say that in the countries technically called capitalist, capitalism is not a belief that is desperately defended as a myth of concern. It is otherwise with "democracy," as most of us take in, through the pores of our primary education, a concerned belief in democracy as an inclusive social ideal that works toward giving equal rights to all citizens. Among those for whom democracy is a genuine myth of concern and capitalism not one, many feel that in America the democratic ideal was kidnapped at the beginning by a social movement which was really oligarchical, based on various forms of exploitation, including slavery and later racism, and hence exclusive, which built up a hysterically competitive economy on a thunderous cannonade of systematic lying, and finally began to spill over into imperialistic crusades like the Vietnam war. The lunatic obsessiveness of a foreign policy that keeps on making aggressive gestures at a time when any serious war would wipe out the human race carries the situation beyond the point of normal loyalties. The result is that many people, especially in the under-thirty age group, feel alienated from their own society, to the point of what is sometimes called an identity crisis.

As a result there has been a strongly revived sense of concern, which finds much of its focus in the universities. The universities are the social centres of the myth of freedom, and are, by necessity, devoted to the virtues of the truth of correspondence, including objectivity and detachment. These are felt to be insufficient virtues in the face of a direct threat to human survival, and hence there is a strong desire to transform the university, in particular, into a society of concern, like a church or political party. One reason for this curious and confused situation is that education itself, during the last century, has taken on many of the features of a myth of concern: compulsory and universal schooling, combined with the attempt to instil concerned social attitudes as part of the educational process (saluting the flag and the like), have turned the schools into a kind of secular church. We note in passing that whenever, in society, the sense of concern receives a shock, whenever the sense of a solid social order that we accept and go along with is weakened, we realize how primary social concern is. If concern is damaged, that damage must be patched up first, no matter what happens to the virtues fostered by reason and evidence.

It seems obvious that, for people on this continent at least, the cure for the identity crisis just mentioned is the recovery of their own revolutionary and democratic myth of concern. A number of radicals may profess a democratic mythology who are actually fascinated by some monopolistic myth that permits of no dissent, and others may look to whatever Marxist leadership appears to be still in the age of innocence, like that of Che Guevara. But this search for a heroic ideal just beyond the frontier is itself a central part of American mythology, and, as with the pool of Narcissus, the real source of its attractiveness is not difficult to find. Certainly there is a tremendous radical force in American culture, in Whitman's *Democratic Vistas,* in Thoreau's *Walden* and *Civil Disobedience,* in Jefferson's view of local self-determination, in Lincoln's conception of the Civil War as a revolution against the inner spirit of slavery, which could give a very different social slant to the American myth of concern. Ezra Pound, for all his crankiness, was trying to portray something of this innate radicalism in his

John Adams Cantoes. There is also of course a right wing that would like to make the American way of life a closed myth, but its prospects at the moment do not seem bright.

Thirty years ago, during the depression, the last thing that anyone would have predicted was the rise of anarchism as a revolutionary force. It seemed to have been destroyed by Stalinist Communism once and for all. But we seem to be in an anarchist age, and need to retrace our steps to take another look at our historical situation. One reason why the radical mood of today is so strongly anarchist, in America, is that the American radical tradition just referred to, especially in Jefferson and Thoreau, shows many affinities with the decentralizing and separatist tendencies of anarchism, in striking contrast to orthodox Marxism, which had very little in the American tradition to attach itself to. There are some curious parallels between the present and the nineteenth-century American scene, between contemporary turn-on sessions and nineteenth-century ecstatic revivalism, between beatnik and hippie communes and some of the nineteenth-century Utopian projects; and the populist movements at the turn of the century showed the same revolutionary ambivalence, tending equally to the left or to the right, that one sees today. Again, today's radical has inherited the heroic gloom of existentialism, with its doctrine that all genuine commitment begins in the revolt of the individual personality against an impersonal or otherwise absurd environment. The conception of the personal as inherently a revolutionary force, which, as we saw, began in a Christian context in Kierkegaard, was developed in a secular one by French writers associated with the resistance against the Nazis, this resistance being the direct ancestor of the more localized revolutionary movements of our day.

The emphasis on individuality makes it possible for contemporary anarchism to absorb more cultural elements than the

Stalinism of the last generation seemed able to absorb. One of these is a middle-class disillusionment with the values of what is called an affluent society. This kind of disaffection is not, like orthodox Marxism, directed at the centres of economic power: it is rather a psychologically based revolution, a movement of protest directed at the anxieties of privilege. It does not fight for workers against exploiters so much as attack and ridicule the work ethic itself. It does not see Negro segregation or the Vietnam war merely as by-products of a class struggle: it sees the fears and prejudices involved in these issues as primary, and the insecurity that inspires them as the real enemy.

Here the radical mood of our time attaches itself to a revolutionary movement that started up in the nineteenth century, mainly in France, which had little in common with other revolutionary movements of its time except its opposition to the bourgeois ascendancy. This was what the nineteenth century called Bohemianism, the way of life pursued by many creative artists, both poets and painters, in opposition to the mores of their society. The *vie de Bohème* was more hedonistic and freer in its sexual standards than its more respectable rival, and it carried on a guerrilla campaign against the kind of middle-class anxieties that are usually expressed by the word "decency." The symbols of its social opposition included drugs, specifically hashish, which is prominent in the imagery of Baudelaire, and a not-so-sweet disorder in the dress ("je m'encrapule le plus possible," said Rimbaud). When this movement revived in the twentieth century, it expanded from the arts into the expression of a revolutionary life-style, for which the spokesman was Freud rather than Marx. This was hardly a role that Freud would have envisaged for himself, but in the beat movement of the fifties, even in their hippie successors, one sees a curious effort to define a social proletariat in Freudian rather than Marxist terms. From its point of view, bourgeois society is a repressive anxiety-structure which is particularly disturbed by the sexual instinct, hence the renewal of society is bound up with the emancipating of that instinct, though this also involves associating it with the creative process.

The addition of a sexual and erotic component to the revolutionary scene fulfills the original revolutionary prophecies of Blake and Shelley, for whom all political freedom was inextricably bound up with what Blake calls "an improvement of sensual enjoyment." Another element in this is what we may call a kind of "sartor resartus" situation. In the symbolism of Carlyle's book, clothes reveal the body, by enabling it to become publicly visible, and at the same time they conceal and disguise it. When society is properly functioning, according to Carlyle, its institutions are a clothing that fits it and reveals its form; when society has outgrown its institutions and is due for a radical change, those institutions have become merely a disguise. In the present mood of concern, the "establishment" seems to wear an outward semblance of liberal tolerance, expressed in the university and elsewhere, but the naked reality underneath it is a death-wish.

The impetus toward revealing nakedness, which often takes very literal forms, goes in both directions. In one direction is the attempt to tear off the disguises of tolerance and good will, of rationalization and liberal rhetoric, from the "establishment," and in the other there is the popularity of encounter groups and similar devices for uncovering one's "real" emotions. The ultimate result is assumed to be a confrontation of innocent with guilty nakedness. Prudery, it is felt, is an important element in ruling-class mythology for many reasons, one of which is a feeling that sex should be concealed and subordinated because it is something equally accessible to the working classes. Hence the shock tactics of "bad" words and an explicit emphasis on sexuality in radicalism. These shock tactics have already largely accomplished, I should think, one of their original aims, which was to change the focus of the obscene expression. The celebrated four-letter words raise few eyebrows today, because the taboo on them never was based on much more than reflex. The real obscenities of our time, the words that no self-respecting person would seriously use, are the words that express hatred or contempt for people of different religion or nationality or skin color, and disapproval of such words is based on a more solid idea of what is socially dangerous.

A revolutionary movement of this partly psychological kind is one in which the arts can play a central and functional role. This is the point at which the literary critic's specific interests enter the contemporary social scene. The growth of a new sense of concern brings with it the urgent necessity of understanding, not merely its psychology or historical causation, but its mythical and poetic language. The greater relevance of the arts to social protest today is connected with another cultural fact of central importance in our present argument. This is the quite sudden revival of oral culture, at least in the North American and European democracies. Oral culture had been fostered a good deal in Communist countries, where in any case the traditions of oral poetry had been much more active. But for us it is a new experience to think of poetry as consisting not so much of a small group of great poets as of a kind of diffused creative energy, much of which takes quite ephemeral forms. It used to be assumed that every creative effort worthy the name was aiming at permanence, and so was really addressed to posterity, but this notion does not have the prestige it once had. A fair amount of this creative energy takes the form of a poetry read or recited to listening groups which is close to improvisation, usually has some kind of musical accompaniment or background, and includes commentary on current social issues. Wyndham Lewis's contempt for the "dithyrambic spectator" seems very remote in the age of folk singers: we are once again in a culture of formulaic units and semi-improvised "happenings," where the role of the audience is of primary importance, and which demands some consolidation of social opinion. We shall not, I hope, go so far as to retribalize our culture completely around formulaic units, as China is now doing with the thoughts of Chairman Mao. But a similar oral context, and a similar appeal to immediate emotional response, is obviously reappearing in our literature.

When I began teaching, a generation ago, literature had become so assimilated to a writing culture that it was being looked at in reverse, and taught the wrong way round. Poetry is at the centre of literature; literary prose, in novels and plays and the like, forms the periphery; outside that again is utilitarian prose, the use of words for non-literary purposes. Educational theory assumed that literature was first of all an art of communication, interpreting the word communication of course in anti-imaginative terms. So its centre of gravity was utilitarian prose, which moved on to literary prose by way of relaxation, and finally, with the greatest reluctance, approached poetry as though it were boiling oil. Students were told that the conventionalizing of speech known as prose, which is actually a very difficult and sophisticated convention, was in fact the natural way to talk and to think; hence they were compelled to compose sentences in what for them was a dead language, with nothing of the actual rhythms of speech in it. However, by the time they reached the university they had finally become more or less convinced that prose really was the language of ordinary speech, though they still could not write it and seldom or never spoke it, and that poetry was a perverse way of distorting ordinary prose statements. Educators today appear to be as ignorant as ever, but their victims are less helpless. They have been educating themselves, partly through the film, with its unparalleled power of presenting things in terms of symbol and archetype, and partly through the oral tradition of popular contemporary poetry. (Again, a generation ago, such a phrase as "popular contemporary poetry" would hardly have made sense.) As a result many students have begun to think of poetic imagery and symbolism as a relatively normal form of thought and speech.

Along with this, and partly as a result of the influence of science fiction, there has grown up a new tolerance for schematic patterns in thinking, of a kind that, as we saw earlier, is deeply congenial to poetry. Astrology, Tarot cards, the I Ching, maverick writers like Velikowski or Gurdjieff, all have their student following; and even more orthodox thinkers can make use of schematic constructs, such as the "culinary triangle" of Lévi-Strauss, that they could hardly have got away with a generation ago. Then again, folk singers often make a quite uninhibited use of mythological, even Biblical, imagery. A line from an early ballad of Bob Dylan's, "There are no truths outside the garden of Eden," may make the central thesis of this essay more intelligible to some of its readers: certainly it makes *Paradise Lost* easier to teach to students familiar with it. This allusiveness is all the more remarkable in that while critics tend increasingly to read poetry by its symbolic "underthought," folk singers and other poets with a listening audience have to make a surface of explicit statement a part of their communication as well.

All this does not mean that a great age of poetry is about to dawn upon us: it means rather the opposite, an absorption of the poetic habit of mind into ordinary experience. The situation is so new that not all its social implications are clear yet. It is still not quite realized that the closer an art is to improvisation, the more it depends on a rigorous convention, as we see in the *commedia dell' arte*. The oral poet is concerned with the ritualized acts, or what Yeats calls the ceremony of innocence, around which social activity revolves in an oral culture. Both oral poetry and the life it reflects rely on a spontaneity which has a thoroughly predictable general convention underlying it. It is consistent with this kind of culture that young people should be concerned, in McLuhan's formulaic phrase, more with roles than with goals, with a dramatic rather than a teleological conception of social function. One result of this has been a concerted effort to break down the distinction between art and life, between stage and audience, drama and event or "happening," display and participation, social role and individual life-style. We thus have, among other things, new forms of social activity which are really improvised symbolic dramas. An example that I witnessed recently was the extraordinary sleepwalking ritual of the "people's park" crisis in Berkeley in the summer of 1969. Here a vacant lot with a fence around it became assimilated to the archetype of the expulsion from Eden, dramatizing the conflict of the democratic community and the oligarchical conspiracy in a pastoral mode related to some common conventions of the Western story. A student editorial informed us that the lot was "covered with blood" because, like all the rest of the land in North America, it had been stolen from the Indians (murder of Abel archetype). The expelling angels in this symbolism were (as in Blake's version of it) demonic, and the police, with their helmets and bayonets and gas masks, were endeavouring, with considerable success, to represent the demonic in its popular science fiction form, of robots or bug-eyed monsters from outer space.

But while the role solves the problem of sincerity, as the actor's sincerity consists in putting on his show and not in believing what he says, it does not solve the greater problem of identity. The role is usually a part in someone else's play, and much radical idealism wavers between the desire to do one's own thing and the desire to surrender unconditionally to some externally imposed social programme. All we can clearly see so far is that, first, the revival of oral culture and the growth of a radical sense of social concern are part of the same process. Second, a society in which the distinction between work of art and social event frequently breaks down is clearly one in which a literary critic cannot ignore the social context of his subject.

The immediate social context of this new verbal culture is provided by the communication media. All these media have a close connection with the centres of social authority and reflect their anxieties. In socialist countries they reflect the anxiety of the political establishment to retain power; in the United States they reflect the anxiety of the economic establishment to keep production running. As Joyce realized, the twentieth century is pre-eminently the age of the *perce-oreille,* the steady insinuating of suggested social attitudes and responses that comes pouring from the active mouth of A into the passive ear of B. Wherever we turn, there is the same implacable voice, unctuous, caressing, inhumanly complacent, selling us food, cars, political leaders, ideologies, culture, contemporary issues, and remedies against the migraine we get from listening to it. As I have tried to suggest by this list, it is not only the voice we hear that haunts us, but the voice that goes on echoing in our minds, forming our social attitudes, our habits of speech, our processes of thought.

If people did not resent and resist this they would not be human, and the nightmares about society turning into an insect state would come true. The democracies are at a peculiar disadvantage, in comparison with the Marxist empires, in that they cannot suggest a socially participatory role for their listeners. They have to treat them primarily as consumers, and hence as objects to be stimulated. As with erotic stimulation, or rather as with other forms of erotic stimulation, there is a large element of mechanical and involuntary response. But there is resentment too, a resentment which turns to panic when it becomes obviously impossible to escape, and it seems clear that a good deal of the shouting and smashing and looting and burning of our times is to be connected with this panic. We hear of meetings broken up and speakers howled down by organized gangs; we try to phone from a public booth and find the telephone torn out; we read of hijacked planes and of bombs in letter boxes; hoodlums go berserk in summer resorts and adolescents scream all the words they know that used to be called obscene. All such acts, however silly or vicious in themselves, are acts of counter-communication, acts noisy enough or outrageous enough to shout down that voice and spit at that image, if only for a few moments.

But hysterical violence is self-defeating, not merely because it is violence but because, as counter-communication, it can only provoke more of what it attacks. Every outbreak of violence releases more floods of alarm, understanding, deep reservations, comment in perspective, denunciation, concern, sympathy, analysis, and reasoned argument. In other words, and other and other and other words, it develops more and more and more communication from talking A to listening B, while violence, however long it lasts, continues to go around in the circles of lost direction. There is a vaguely Freudian notion that there is something therapeutic in releasing inhibitions; but it is clear that releasing inhibitions is quite as compulsive, repetitive and hysterical an operation as the repressing of them.

All this is very puzzling to, say, an advertiser who does not understand that a television set is not only his way of reaching his market, but his market's way of looking at him. If the viewer is black and the advertiser presents a vision of a white society gorging itself on privilege and luxury goods, the results can be explosive. Many other forms of contemporary "unrest" seem to me to have much to do with the fact that verbal communication is a one-way street. In university demonstrations it has been noticed that a good many students acquire their deeper convictions after the newsreel cameras arrive: they express their aggressiveness, in other words, by getting on the other side of the television set. The decline in the prestige of the more conventional types of monologue, such as lectures in universities and sermons in churches, doubtless has similar origins.

The instinctive resistance offered to mass communication is apathy, but the communicating techniques of our times have learned how to get past apathy, and no longer find it a real barrier. Much more strenuous forms of resistance then develop: drugs, for instance, which may promise genuinely new sensory experiences, of a kind that mass media cheat us out of and that the socially approved narcotics fail to provide; or rock music, which wraps up the listener in an impermeable cloak of noise. Still more significant is the political resistance. The age which has achieved an instant delivery of news from all parts of the world is also the age in which the strongest political development is separatism. If the world is becoming a global village, we should not forget that the primary characteristics of village life include cliques, feuds and impassable social barriers.

The direction of most of the technological developments of our time has been towards greater introversion. The automobile, the passenger aeroplane, the movie, the television set, the highrise apartment, are more introverted than their predecessors, and the result is increased alienation and a decline in the sense of festivity, the sense of pleasure in belonging to a community. Even our one technically festive season, Christmas, is an introverted German Romantic affair, based on a myth of retreat into the cave of a big Dickensian family life of a type that hardly exists any more. The same introversion comes into a good deal of contemporary art, with its abstract monotony, its rejection of the external world, its neo-neolithic geometrizing. The one advantage of an introverted situation is privacy; but for us the growing introversion goes along with a steady decrease in privacy. This means that the psychological conditions of life, whatever the physical conditions, become increasingly like those of life in a prison, where there is introversion but no privacy and no real community. Against such a background, the growth of a sense of festivity connected with poetry and music, however noisy or strident, could be an encouraging sign.

The revival of oral culture in our day has been variously interpreted, and one interpretation, suggested and strongly influenced by McLuhan, is that print represents a "linear" and time-bound approach to reality, and that the electronic media, by reviving the oral tradition, have brought in a new "simultaneous" or mosaic form of understanding. Contemporary unrest, in this view, is part of an attempt to adjust to a new situation and break away from the domination of print. We saw in the first section, however, that the difference between the linear and the simultaneous is not a difference between two kinds of media, but a difference between two mental operations within all media, that there is always a linear response followed by a simultaneous one whatever the medium. For words, the document, the written or printed record, is the technical device that makes the critical or simultaneous response possible. The document is the model of all teaching, because it is infinitely patient, repeating the same words however often one consults it, and the spatial focus it provides makes it possible to return on the experience, a repetition of the kind that underlies all genuine education. The document is also the focus of a community of readers, and while this community may be restricted to one group for centuries, its natural tendency is to expand over the community as a whole. Thus it is only writing that makes democracy technically possible. It is significant that our symbolic term for a tyrant is "dictator," that is, an uninterrupted oral speaker.

The domination of print in Western society, then, has not simply made possible the technical and engineering efficiency of that society, as McLuhan emphasizes; it has also created all the conditions of freedom within that society: democratic government, universal education, tolerance of dissent, and (because the book individualizes its audience) the sense of the importance of privacy, leisure, and freedom of movement. Democracy and book culture are interdependent, and the rise of oral and visual media represents, not a new order to adjust to, but a subordinate order to be contained. What the oral media have brought in is, by itself, anarchist in its social affinities. They suggest the primitive and tribal conditions of a pre-literate culture, and to regard them as a new and autonomous order would lead, once again, to adopting a cyclical view of history, resigning ourselves to going around the circle again, back to conditions that we have long ago outgrown. As remarked above, the circle is the symbol of lost direction, and, because the future *qua* future is only the analogy of the past, it is also the only possible form of an untried direction. In every generation the inexperience of youth revolts against the wasted experience of its elders, and repeats the cycle in its turn. In the present age this situation has gigantically expanded, but the main effect of the new media is to turn the wheel faster. So far from encouraging a shift from linear and fragmented to simultaneous and versatile response, the electronic media have intensified the sense of a purely linear experience which can only be repeated or forgotten. Hence the "linear" panic about keeping up, getting with it, meeting the demands of a changed situation, and the like, is similarly intensified.

It is all very well to say that the medium is the message, but as we seem to get much the same message from all the media, it follows that all media, within a given social environment like that of the Soviet Union or the United States, are much the same medium. This is because the real communicating media are still, as they always have been, words, images, and rhythms, not the electronic gadgets that convey them. The differences among the gadgets, whether they are of high or low definition and the like, must be of great technical interest, especially to those working with them, but they are clearly of limited social importance. If a country goes to war after developing television, the use of a "cooler" medium does not, unfortunately, cool off the war. The identification of medium and message is derived from the arts: painting, for instance, has no "message" except the medium of painting itself. But it is a false analogy to apply this principle to interested, or baited-trap, communication from A to B. There, one identifies form and content only as long as one is relatively unconscious of the form and still bemused by its novelty: but in direct communication, as soon as one becomes aware of the form, the content separates from it.

I have spoken of the anxiety of continuity in society, which is not only a social feeling, but reappears in the personal life as well. What it is anxious about is the threat to one's identity which is contained in experience. There is all the variety in moods, so great that one often hardly seems to be the same person throughout a day; there is the variety of social relationships which compels us to change our idioms of expression as often as our clothes; there is the variety of opinions and attitudes suggested to us by discussion and the effect of other personalities. One sets up a pattern of repetition, of habit, custom, convention, doing what one has always done, in order to preserve the feeling that one is the same person throughout one's experience, that behind the caprice of mood is consistency of purpose, behind the change of opinion consistency of principle, and that such consistency is the containing form of one's real existence.

Such a consistency operates on two levels: a superficial level in which habit and custom become ends in themselves, and a deeper level in which they serve their real purpose of creating a constant sense of identity. Thus if an opinion that one has held all one's life becomes obviously inadequate, clinging to the opinion in order to resist the thought of change is a superficial consistency, discarding or modifying it a sign of a deeper consistency of attitude. Similarly in the arts: once a convention is established, the writers or painters who follow it closely become quickly fashionable. An original artist comes along, and we say he is unconventional, that he represents a discontinuity with tradition. But if he is genuinely original he will soon show a traditional quality, though on a deeper level of tradition. Shallow and deep consistency represent two different and opposed uses of the memory. A consistency motivated only by the fear of change uses the memory to live in the past, preserve the status quo in the present, and make the future as predictable as possible. For a more organic consistency memory becomes practice memory, using habit and repetition to develop skills and learning processes. Whatever virtues we have, such as honesty or truthfulness, are also consistent habits in this sense.

Remembering that it is the electronic media which most strongly suggest the linear and the fragmented, we can see that they help to create a powerful sense of discontinuity in society. Their influence is reinforced by muddled educational theories which do not distinguish the two forms of memory in learning, and so confuse the repetition underlying the learning process itself with "mere learning by rote" and the like. When the sense of a continuum of identity in life is weakened, individual life breaks down into a discontinuous sequence of experiences, in which the sexual experiences loom up very prominently. The reason why they do become prominent is that one's sexual life, as such, is not so much individual as generic: people may love in individual ways, but copulation in itself, like birth and death, is of the species. I spoke of Kierkegaard's use of Leporello's catalogue of mistresses in *Don Giovanni* as a symbol of the "aesthetic," or falsely individualized, attitude to experience, and of course there is a sense in which all Don Giovanni's mistresses are the same woman, or the same female object. In the mechanical sexuality of so much contemporary entertainment there comes back into our culture something of the fetishism that we have in that quaint little paleolithic object called the Venus of Willendorf, all belly and teats and gaping vulva, but no face. The confusion between the physically intimate and the genuinely personal is parallel to, and doubtless related to, the confusion between the introverted and the creative experience in the drug cults.

In universities today the demand for "relevance" has two main sources. One is the sense of the threat to identity created by the discontinuity in contemporary experience; the other (because of course the sense of identity is social as well as individual) is the feeling that one's life is not related to a sufficiently articulate myth of concern, and so lacks an essential dimension of its meaning. We notice how the demand for relevance reflects the inner drive of all concerned thinking to become encyclopaedic, covering every aspect of human life and destiny. From this point of view, scholarship, in the arts and sciences, seems to reinforce the threat to identity. For scholarship is intensely pluralistic, continually forming pockets of research which are sealed off even from their nearest neighbours. Again, while it begins by being impersonal in a good sense, depending on an intellectual honesty that refuses to manipulate evidence, it seems to be easy for it to lose its sense of social perspective, and so become impersonal in the bad sense of being indifferent to human values.

It is at this point that the distinction between closed and open mythologies becomes crucial. A certain amount of contemporary agitation seems to be beating the track of the "think with your blood" exhortations of the Nazis a generation ago, for whom also "relevance" (*Zweckwissenschaft, u.s.w.*) was a constant watchword. Such agitation aims, consciously or unconsciously, at a closed myth of concern, which is thought of as already containing all the essential answers, at least potentially, so that it contains the power of veto over scholarship and imagination. Marcuse's notion of "repressive tolerance," that concerned issues have a right and a wrong side, and that those who are simply right need not bother tolerating those who are merely wrong, is typical of the kind of hysteria that an age like ours throws up. That age is so precariously balanced, however, that a closed myth can only maintain a static tyranny until it is blown to pieces, either externally in war or internally through the explosion of what it tries to suppress.

A society with an open mythology has to recognize the autonomy of scholarship, along with its necessary pluralism and specialization, and recognize also that scholarship contains a power of veto over any aspect of any concerned mythology, as it may at any time provide evidence that contradicts widely held tenets. Again, as noted, it has to release the language of concern itself, allowing the creative imagination in its artists to follow whatever paths the conventions of the arts in their time suggest. Literature, left to itself, follows the encyclopaedic pattern of concern, and covers the entire range of imaginative possibilities, although of course every age stresses some conventions more than others. It has also to recognize that a power-structure or establishment, at any given moment, does not manifest the real form of that society, but only its transient appearance; hence all genuine effort at social change aims, not at creating "another society," or even a "new society," but at releasing the real form of the society it is in.

Preserving a myth of freedom along with a myth of concern in society is difficult and dangerous, for while a society with an open mythology is obviously better for human life than a society with a closed one, yet an open mythology is by no means a panacea. Not only is there a constant pressure within society to close its mythology, from both radical and conservative wings, but the efforts to keep it open have to be strenuous, constant, delicate, unpopular, and above all largely negative. When it comes to meeting the threat to identity, a myth of freedom seems very ineffective in comparison with the narcotic charm of a closed myth of concern, with its instant, convinced and final answers. It takes time to realize that these answers are not only not genuine answers, but that only the questions can be genuine, and all such answers cheat us out of our real birthright, which is the right to ask the questions.

For a closed myth of concern, the question of relevance could hardly be easier to answer: anything is relevant that is relevant to it. It is equally easy to apply, for this kind of relevance relates the subject to the student: the slithering downward way of mindless educators, not the flinty uphill path of relating the student to the subject, which is the way of genuine education. For the myth of freedom, no built-in or inherent relevance exists in any subject: only the student himself can establish the relevance of what he studies, and being a student means accepting the responsibility for doing so. To make such a commitment in the midst of the confusion of our time is an act of historical significance, civilization being the sane man's burden. To return to Kant's use of the phrase which is my title, those who are paralyzed either by the dogmatism of unliberated concern or by the skepticism of unconcerned freedom have to be written off, however large a majority they may form. It is only those who have embarked on some critical path who are living in the history of their time.

Seven

Social mythology is polarized by two mythical conceptions, the conception of the social contract and the conception of the Utopia or ideal state. These two principles of contract and Utopia descend historically, as myths, from their Christian predecessors, the alienation myth of the fall of man and the fulfilment myth of the City of God. Behind the contract myth in particular we can catch a glimpse of the legal metaphor in the Christian tradition expressed by the word "testament" to describe the structure of the Bible, where God voluntarily binds himself to a contract (*diatheke*, not a *syntheke* or contract on equal terms) with man. The contract myth begins as a fiction about a transfer of social authority in the distant past, but it soon becomes clear that a contract myth is an attempt to account for the present structure of society as it presents itself to the myth-maker.

Modern contract mythology begins with Edmund Burke, for whom a society's real contract is its existing structure of authority. Before we are born, we are predestined to a certain social position at a certain point in time; before we have any personality we have a social context. Because we are given our loyalties before we are capable of choosing them, to try to reject what one is already committed to can only lead to chaos, both in personal and social life. Further, it is the permanence and continuity of social institutions, including church and state, that not only civilizes man, but adds the dimension of historical significance to his life. A similar association of social concern with historical continuity appears in T. S. Eliot close to our own day.

I have so far said nothing about the secular or national myths of concern, which had always been there, but became immensely powerful in the nineteenth century. As myths, they are very largely interchangeable, and they are all simple forms of contract mythology: because we have been born British or German or French or what not, the constituted authority of that society has a right not only to our unquestioned loyalty but, in time of war, to our lives. In our day nationalism usually has to sell itself under some more universal label to make much appeal.

The weak spot in the conservative emphasis on the contract, on playing the hand dealt to one at birth, so to speak, is the uncritical element in it. Being involuntarily born into a certain nation seems hardly enough to compel one to adopt the maxim "my country right or wrong." The primary justification for authority, in the conservative view, is the fact that it is there, and this makes it difficult to distinguish reality from appearance in society, what authority actually is from what it seems or pretends to be. If we compare Burke on this subject with Paine, we can see how Burke's position practically forces him to speak of the facade of society as though it were society, as though greed and snobbery and injustice and superstition played no essential role in, for instance, maintaining the ascendancy of the aristocracy. We see a trivial form of the same desire to identify social reality and appearance in the passive or negative concern of the person who automatically switches over to situation comedy as soon as his television set begins to talk about public affairs or education. For such people the fantasies of advertising are not simply part of an ironic game, but are rather a form of drug culture.

The more serious conservative acceptance of the social contract throws a strong emphasis on what is now called "commitment" or "engagement." These are not only largely uncritical attitudes, but also somewhat humorless: their instinct is to rationalize whatever they find existing in society, instead of recognizing anomalies or absurdities in it. Commitment and engagement are attitudes that imply the superiority of the continuum of society to the person who is caught up by it, even if his original commitment was a voluntary choice. The authority of the social contract however is a *de facto* authority: it lacks a genuinely ideal dimension, and so keeps ideals in an empty world of wish or hope or promise, at best in a vague and unspecified future. Thus the complete acceptance of the contract, conceived as the existing structure of authority in society, can only end either in resigned cynicism or in the identifying of reality and appearance just mentioned.

Hence there grows up in society a radical or Utopian social view, which has steadily increased, not merely in strength but in authority, during the last century. The radical view of the contract focusses on the uncritical element in it, and feels that maturity and development are a matter of becoming aware of our social conditioning, and so of making a choice between presented and discovered loyalties. The only real loyalty, from this point of view, is the voluntary or self-chosen loyalty, which is often loyalty to a social ideal not yet in existence. This transfer of loyalty from one's native society to another society still to be constructed creates an intensely Utopian state of mind, which attaches its loyalty to an ideal, and then works toward gathering enough force around this ideal to smash the existing contract, and thereby become a new *de facto* authority. As such it postulates an *ideal* contract, buried underneath the actual one, which the society of the future is to restore or manifest.

In our day the Marxist revolutionary myth is the Utopian counterpart to the more conservative and nationalistic conceptions of society, including the progressive gradualism referred to earlier. When Engels contrasted Utopian and "scientific" socialism he was really completing the Utopian conception. In a world like ours a limited Utopia in a restricted or enclosed space is an empty fantasy: Utopia must be a world-wide transformation of the whole social order or it is nothing. But for it to be this it must be conceived, not as an *a priori* rational construct, as in most Utopian romances, but as the *telos* of history, the end to which history points. The "scientific" element in Engels's socialism, then, is a religious or concerned belief in the teleology of history. We see this in the intensely teleological nature of Marxist revolutionary tactics, in which every strike or demonstration is one more step in the advance to the final takeover.

But of course this potential society of the future will also demand commitment, of a much more intense kind. The radical Utopian attitude recognizes anomalies and absurdities in existing society, but its own loyalty is still less critical, even more eager to rationalize, more impatient with dissent, more anxious to suppress the perception of anomalies in itself. No myth of freedom can ever emerge out of this situation: instead of getting more liberalism and tolerance out of the conflict of concerns we eventually get less, as each side progressively identifies these qualities with the disguises of its enemy. We have noticed how frequently a myth of concern rests on a false version of history, or, at best, on a very strained interpretation of it. The Utopian vision of a future classless society is similarly distorted, as ideals projected into the future get us involved in a pernicious means-to-an-end process which ignores the fact that means cannot lead to ends, because they condition and eventually replace those ends. One suspects that there must be some reality in the present moment of which this future-directed fiction is the shadow.

If we look at the greatest writers who deal with ideal societies, such as Plato, More, Locke or Rousseau, we begin to suspect that they are not really writing about contracts or Utopias at all, but about the theory of education. It is clearly education that these four writers at least most care about, and their fictions about what happened in a remote past or might conceivably happen in a remote future or other place are expendable. The institutions to which man is attached are mainly products of concern, and they form the complex of temporal authority. He may spend his whole life in this context, but an educated man in a complex society also becomes aware, through his education, of another kind of authority, which has only an internal or inherent compulsion: the authority of the rational argument, the accurate measurement, the repeatable experiment, the compelling imagination. Out of this comes the community of those who appeal to the largely non-mythical features of civilization, the features which suggest an environment outside the immediate society and its enemies, and which form the basis of the myth of freedom. This community constitutes a genuine *de jure* or spiritual authority in society. The ideal state, then, is a projection into the future of a source of spiritual authority, founded on the myth of freedom, that sits in the middle of society, and which I shall call the educational contract.

The educational contract is the process by which the arts and sciences, with their methods of logic, experiment, amassing of evidence and imaginative presentation, actually operate as a source of spiritual authority in society. What they create is a free authority, something coherent enough to help form a community, but not an authority in the sense of being able to apply external compulsion. The sense of the permanence and continuity of social institutions, so powerful in Burke's day, is now greatly weakened, along with the belief that they are any better for being permanent. There still remains the continuity of the arts and sciences. This is not a gradualist continuity: every subject of knowledge has gone through a long series of revolutionary transformations. It is rather the form of continuity that we have called deep or organic consistency, and this consistency is something that everyone experiences in his own education, as he recapitulates the earlier stages of the subjects he studies.

The conception of an educational contract was the main contribution made by the development of educational theory in nineteenth-century England, which is also usually regarded as one of the world's greatest eras of liberal thought. The educational contract is the area of free thought and discussion at the centre of John Stuart Mill's view of liberty, and which he thought of as a kind of intellectual counterpart of Parliament. It differs from Parliament, for Mill, in that the liberals can never have a majority, which is why democracy has to function as an illogical but deeply humane combination of majority rule and minority right. In Arnold the educational contract is called culture, and Arnold is explicit about culture's being the source of genuine authority in society and at the same time operating in a Utopian direction by breaking down the barriers of class conflict. Newman draws a distinction between liberal and useful knowledge, in which only the former belongs

to the educational contract, but this is really a difference between two aspects of knowledge rather than two kinds of
knowledge.

The educational contract is what the university in society
primarily stands for. The conceptions of Mill, Arnold and
Newman are wider than the university, but the university is
their engine room, and free authority can last only so long as
the university keeps operating. The university is its centre, not
as an institution, but as the place where the appeal to reason,
experiment, evidence and imagination is constantly going on.
It is not and never can be a concerned organization, like a
church or a political party, and the tactics of trying to revolu-
tionize society by harassing and bedevilling the university are
not serious tactics. Of course the university is easy to harass,
hence doing so gives a false sense of accomplishment.

Going back to our writers on Utopias, we notice that, for
example, Socrates in the *Republic* is not interested in setting
up his ideal state anywhere: what he is interested in is the
analogy between his ideal state and the structure of the wise
man's mind. The latter is an absolute dictatorship of reason
controlling desire through the will, and these three elements
correspond to the philosopher-king, soldiers, and artisans of
the political myth. The ideal state exists, so far as we know,
only in such wise minds, who will obey its laws whatever society they are actually living in. In More's *Utopia*, the narrator
Hythlodaye is a revolutionary communist, but More himself
suggests using the knowledge of Utopia rather as a means of
bringing about an improvement in European society from
within. Thus the real Utopia becomes the social vision of the
wise counsellor's mind, founded on a humanistic education.
Plato and More realize that while the wise man's mind is
rigidly disciplined, and while the nature state is ordered, we
cannot take the analogy between the disciplined mind and the

disciplined state too literally: if we did we should get the most frightful tyranny in the latter. The real Utopia is an individual goal, of which the disciplined society is an allegory. The end of commitment and engagement is the community: the logical end of detachment is the individual. But this is not an antithesis: the genuine individual is so only after he has come to terms with his community. This is the reason way the individual goal is symbolized by a political analogy. The Utopian ideal points beyond the individual to a condition in which, as in Kant's kingdom of ends, society and individual are no longer in conflict, but have become different aspects of the same human body.

We do not now think of the wise man's mind as a dictatorship of reason, of which an authoritarian society could be an allegory: in fact we do not think about the wise man's mind at all. We think rather, in more Freudian terms, of a mind in which a principle of sanity is fighting for its life against a thundering herd of chaotic impulses, which cannot be simply suppressed but must be frequently indulged and humored, allowed to have their say however perverse or infantile. In short, we think of the mind as a participatory democracy; and our social ideals become, as before, an idealized political allegory of such a mind. In this analogy there is no place for the inner-directed person who resists society, like Socrates, or like More himself, and for that very reason the analogy seems more compelling.

We cannot, therefore, recognize the autonomy of the arts and sciences on the ground that objective truth exists in a Platonic world of forms or a Christian unfallen world which the wise or good man inhabits. We may believe that it exists, but in practice it is a world not to see but to see by, an informing power rather than an objective goal to be attained. It is for this reason that the liberty of the arts, more particularly literature, forms an essential part of the myth of freedom. To liberate the language of concern is to ensure that the whole imaginative range of concern is being expressed in society, instead of being confined to a selected type of imagination which is hitched to the tactics of one social group, as propaganda for it, or what we have called a rhetorical analogue to it.

The chief mythical schemata of the twentieth century were outlined in the nineteenth, and a critic concerned with the stereotypes of social mythology finds little that is essentially new in this field in the century since *Culture and Anarchy*. In that book Arnold, whose thinking is more schematic than he himself realized, speaks of the three classes of society, upper, middle and lower, as elements in the ultimate classless society towards which "culture" leads. So far as they are classes, their jockeying for power hinders and retards the growth of culture: it would have seemed the wildest paradox to Arnold to think of arriving at a classless society through increasing the ascendancy of one of its classes. Reactivating the aristocracy, as Carlyle was urging, would merely create a new barbarism; the dictatorship of the proletariat would reduce society to a "populace," and the ascendancy of the bourgeoisie in Arnold's own Victorian England was producing only Philistinism.

Yet each class contains a classless idea to contribute to culture as a whole, which is genuine only when detached from its class context. The bourgeois class contains the idea of "liberty," that is, the assumption that the well-being of a society is measured by the degree of individual life it permits. Many aspects of this liberty fall outside the scope of the present essay, but the elements in what we have been calling the myth of freedom are central to Arnold's conception of culture, though, as explained earlier, the humanist context of that conception no longer exists. As a class concept, of course, liberty can hardly be distinguished from laissez faire, the liberty to exploit. Hence the necessity for considering also the working-class contribution to culture, which is the idea of equality. Arnold frequently reminded his British middle-class readers that it was possible to pursue liberty to the point of forgetting about equality, just as other writers say of other societies that it is possible to pursue equality to the point of forgetting about liberty.

It appears that the idea of equality forms the nucleus of most myths of concern in our day, in both Marxist and democratic countries. It is not itself a myth of concern, but a concerned feeling entering into every serious myth, whatever its reference. In the democracies there is a deeply concerned opposition charging that democracies are still dominated by oligarchical and exclusivist habits of thought, that the treatment of the black or "third world" elements in democratic society is still not good enough by the standard of equality. There is also a strong feeling in the democracies (held mainly, though not entirely, by a different group of people) that middle-class societies preserve essential elements of freedom which get lost in proletarian movements. The defense of freedom by itself has the disadvantage that the myth of freedom is a secondary and derivative myth, appropriate chiefly to societies that have already attained some success in meeting the primary requirements of concern. Hence those who feel that democratic societies should be dissolved and reconstituted on a basis of total equality find it easy to assume that questions of freedom are not important, or will take care of themselves, or should be postponed and wait their turn. Marxist countries, on the other hand, have begun to develop a fiercely persecuted but steadily growing liberal opposition which sees the real Utopian goal of society as an individualized one.

There is an implicit, if not explicit, link in Arnold's mind between his third class, the aristocracy, and the third revolutionary ideal of fraternity. Just as the class-bound conceptions of liberty and equality lead inevitably to American troops in Cambodia and Russian troops in Czechoslovakia, so a class-bound conception of fraternity could lead only to Nazism and Fascism, with their phony hero cults. But if we detach the fundamental idea of aristocracy, respecting a man because of his birth, from its class context, it becomes the ultimate social ideal of respecting a man because he has been born, because he is there. This dream of a world in which there is no difference between loyalty to society and loyalty to individuals, including one's self, is occasionally glimpsed in literature, in the pastoral tradition, in Rabelais' Abbey of Theleme, in Yeats's lords and ladies of Byzantium, but always with a sense of lurking paradox. In an age dominated by Hegelian and Marxist schematisms of antitheses resolving in a new and wider unity, it may be thought that this ideal society could be the synthesis that will arise in future out of the present form of the struggle of concern and freedom. An older, and perhaps wiser, philosophical tradition tells us that the synthesis never in fact comes into existence, and that antithesis or tension of opposites is the only form in which it can exist.

So we come back to where our critical path began, in the contrast between an existing world and a world which may not exist but is pointed to by the articulate orders of experience, the intelligible world of the thinker and the imaginative world of the artist, which are or seem to be analogies of it. This world is frequently called (in Buddhism, for example) an unborn world, a world that never quite enters existence. Its presence, however, or, more accurately, the lively feeling of its absence, is what accounts for the quality of pleasure in the arts. There is a false form of imaginative pleasure, connected

with what Kierkegaard calls the aesthetic attitude to experience, which is passive, a sense of a pleasantly stimulated subject contemplating an inscrutably beautiful object. This leads
to an idolatry of art, a second-rate pseudo-concern in which
art itself becomes an object of concern, something to be believed in. The genuine form of it brings us face to face with
the myths of concern we have been examining. Pleasure seems
a most unlikely development out of concern, which is so often
only a hairsbreadth away from bigotry and fanaticism, violence
and terror. Yet the poet's role clearly has to do with providing
pleasure, even though all the bogies and demons of obsession
are inside his magic circle.

Myths of concern enable members of a society to hold together, to accept authority, to be loyal to each other and
courageous against attack. Such myths are verbal constructions
designed for specific social purposes. In literature myths are
disinterested: they are forms of human creativity, and as such
they communicate the joy—a more concrete word than pleasure—that belongs to pure creation. They are formed out of
every conceivable horror and iniquity of human life, and yet
an inner exuberance lifts them clear of that life. Literature is
unique among the arts in being able to reflect the world escaped from, in its conventions of tragedy and irony and satire,
along with the world escaped to, in its conventions of pastoral
and romance and comedy.

The world of imagination, from this point of view, is partly
a holiday or Sabbath world where we rest from belief and
commitment, the greater mystery beyond whatever can be
formulated and presented for acceptance. On earth and in
history, Christianity destroyed the belief in the Classical gods,
but the Classical gods promptly went to the imaginative
heaven of poetry, and Venus was perhaps more genuinely
revered in Renaissance Europe, as one of what Emily Dickin-

son calls "our confiscated gods," than she ever was in her temple at Cyprus. As that very wise man J. L. Borges has remarked, literature not only begins in a myth, it also ends in one. He made this remark in connexion with Don Quixote, who begins in the narrowest possible confinement, a neurotic fanaticism, a commitment to a myth of concern that makes no sense, and ends by haunting the imagination of the entire world. One of the mysterious and yet central facts about literature is that it is capable of this kind of growth, growth through space, through time, through all the barriers of belief and of cultural differentiation: and criticism is its growth.

But the arts are witnesses to something more than a rest after labor, however important that may be in itself. At the basis of human existence is the instinct for social coherence, which in our day is trying to escape in some degree from the exclusiveness that in the past has always marked the boundaries of specific myths of concern. Concern by itself can never be entirely free from the clattering of anxiety, the fear of heresy, the hysteria of intolerance and violence. It is the basis of all community, but in itself it cannot distinguish a community from a mob. Above it is individual life, and only the individual is capable of happiness. The basis of happiness is a sense of freedom or unimpeded movement in society, a detachment that does not withdraw; and the basis of that sense of independence is consciousness. It is the articulated worlds of consciousness, the intelligible and imaginative worlds, that are at once the reward of freedom and the guarantee of it. But just as society is never free from hysteria, so individual freedom is never itself entirely free from a privilege that somebody else is partly paying for. It is out of the tension between concern and freedom that glimpses of a third order of experience emerge, of a world that may not exist but completes existence, the world of the definitive experience that poetry urges us to have but which we never quite get. If such a world existed, no individual could live in it, because the society he belongs to is part of himself, including all those who are too cold and hungry and sick ever to get near it. No society, even the smallest and most dedicated community, could live in it, because the innocence needed to live continuously in such a world would require a nakedness far beyond anything that removing one's clothes could reach. If we could live in it, of course, criticism would cease and the distinction between literature and life would disappear, because life itself would then be the continuous incarnation of the creative word.

Notes

Page 13. *"Critique of Pure Reason."* So most translations, though Kant's word is *Weg*, not *Pfad*.

Page 14. "aesthetics." For an opposed view, see F. E. Sparshott, *The Structure of Aesthetics,* Toronto, 1963.

Page 15. "August Boeckh." See *Encyklopädie und Methodologie der philologischen Wissenschaften,* Leipzig, 1877, especially the opening chapter, "Die Idee der Philologie."

Page 16. "Miss Maud Bodkin." *Archetypal Patterns in Poetry,* 1934.

Page 28. "Schiller's terms." I have used these already in a different context in *Anatomy of Criticism* (1957), 35.

Page 34. "Vico." *Scienza Nuova,* etc., translated as *The New Science of Giambattista Vico,* T. G. Bergin and M. H. Fisch, 1948 (rev. 1968). See especially Book Two, "Poetic Wisdom."

Page 35. "paideuma." See Ezra Pound, "Date Line," in *Literary Essays,* ed. T. S. Eliot, 77.

Page 38. "Ahikar." See R. H. Charles, *The Apocrypha and Pseudepigrapha of the Old Testament* (1913), II, 715 ff.

"some scholars." I have been particularly indebted to Albert B. Lord, *The Singer of Tales* (1960); E. A. Havelock, *A Preface to Plato* (1963); Walter J. Ong, *The Presence of the Word* (1967).

Page 42. "writing culture." Of course by this phrase I do not mean simply a culture that uses writing for legal, commercial or religious purposes, but one that publicly and habitually uses writing for its imaginative and intellectual expression. Cf. Harold A. Innis, *The Basis of Communication* (1951), ch. ii.

Page 43. "Richard III." More accurately, the Duke of Gloucester in *Henry VI, Part Three,* V, vi.

Page 54. "Lucretius." *De Rerum Natura,* i, 63 ff.

Page 63. The passage from Roger Ascham is in *The Scholemaster,* II (*English Works of Roger Ascham,* ed. Wright, 1904, 265–6) and from Milton in *Familiar Letters,* 8, tr. David Masson.

Page 65. "Ovid." *Fasti,* vi, 5.

Page 68. "Hopkins." Letter to Alexander Baillie, Jan. 14, 1883.

Page 69. "T. S. Eliot's comparison." From "Conclusion" to *The Use of Poetry and the Use of Criticism* (1933), 151.

Page 85. "as has often been shown." See for example Richard Hofstader, *Social Darwinism in American Thought,* 1944.

Page 91. "Blake." *Jerusalem,* Plate 15.

Page 141. "Rimbaud." Letter to George Izambard, May 13, 1871.

Page 170. "Borges." See *Labyrinths* (1962), 262.